The Abraham Flexner Lectures in Medicine / 1973

Stone Age Crisis

A Psychiatric Appraisal

B. G. Burton-Bradley

VANDERBILT UNIVERSITY PRESS
Nashville, 1975

Frontispiece: Photograph by the author of a traditional village structure in the mountains of the West Sepik District. Migration of able-bodied and young adults, lured away by the cash economy of urban areas, creates village societies largely composed of the very young and the very old.

Dr. Burton-Bradley and the Vanderbilt University Press gratefully acknowledge permission to quote from his publications by the following:

Australian & New Zealand Journal of Psychiatry.
"Papua and New Guinea Transcultural Psychiatry: The First One Thousand Referrals," 3:130-136, 1969. By permission of the editor.

The Medical Journal of Australia.
"The Amok Syndrome in Papua and New Guinea," 1:252-256, 1968; "The New Guinea Prophet: Is the Cultist Always Normal?" 1:124-129, 1970; "Human Sacrifice for Cargo," 2:668-670, 1972; "The Psychiatry of Cargo Cult," 2:388-392, 1973. By permission of the editor.

New Guinea Research Unit, Australian National University.
Mixed-Race Society in Port Moresby. By permission of the publisher.

Library of Congress Cataloging in Publication Data

Burton-Bradley, B. G.
    Stone age crisis.

    (The Abraham Flexner lectures in medicine ; 1973)
    Bibliography.
    Includes Index.
    1. Psychiatry, Transcultural—Papua New Guinea.
I. Title.   II. Series: The Abraham Flexner lectures ; 1973.
[DNLM: 1. Culture.   2. Ethnopsychology.   3. Folklore. BF731 B976sa]
RC451.N332P363   616.8'9'00953   75-4944
ISBN 0-8265-1199-6

To Inge

Contents

ACKNOWLEDGMENTS

This book has its origin in a course of lectures which I had the honor of giving at Vanderbilt while Abraham Flexner Lecturer in 1973. They are reproduced here for the most part as prepared, though in a form somewhat fuller than they were delivered. They are the product of my experience over the last fifteen years, and I have therefore felt free to draw upon certain of my previous publications where this seemed appropriate. The original audience included many psychiatrists, physicians, and other scholars who had little specialist knowledge of Papua New Guinea, and it is my hope that in their expanded form they may interest a similar range of readers, and others. I have accordingly reduced the local idiom to a minimum. All references to mixed-race people are derived from field work performed while I was a student of anthropology at the University of Sydney.

I owe much to many. I am particularly grateful to the people of Papua New Guinea for their tolerance and friendship, and to my mentors Robert Black, Marc Hollender, Neville Parker, and Eric Wittkower, who are in no way responsible for any shortcomings. I have been fortunate in having David Howell Jones and others at the Vanderbilt University Press who took great trouble in preparing the book for the printer. I also had the great help of Paul Symons with the photography, and my secretary Martha Allen in preparing the manuscript.

B. G. BURTON-BRADLEY

Foreword

DR. BURTON-BRADLEY is the acknowledged expert of transcultural psychiatry in the South Pacific. His many degrees, besides medicine, include anthropology, medical psychology, and tropical medicine; and his experiences have been equally diversified. It took a woman, however, to encourage him to undertake the work that has brought him his greatest success. He told me that one day, while he was working in a psychiatric hospital in Australia, his wife suggested that he move, leaving security behind, to follow his interest in transcultural psychiatry. He did as she suggested, moving first to Singapore as Colombo Plan Psychiatrist and then as Lecturer in Psychological Medicine at the University of Malaya. After two years in southeast Asia, he went to Port Moresby to serve as Chief of the Mental Health Services for Papua New Guinea.

To appraise a man's work, it is best to see him function in his own environment. I was fortunate enough to spend several weeks with Dr. Burton-Bradley in New Guinea. When I arrived on a Sunday morning, he met me at the Port Moresby airport and asked if I would join him for Sunday morning brunch with Mrs. Burton-Bradley and some of his neighbors, a pleasant custom among government officials. I was immediately impressed by the high regard and respect his colleagues and friends showed for him. As I visited in New Guinea, my initial impression was confirmed on many other occasions.

Dr. Burton-Bradley's professional duties took him from Port Moresby to the border with West Irian; to the Highlands, where the land is rugged; to Rabaul, a tropical city of 30,000 on one of the many offshore islands. I listened to him interviewing a newly admitted patient, a young man, from a village in the interior, who seemed frightened to find himself not only alone in the capital city, but also in a hospital where he did not know what to expect. Dr. Burton-Bradley was sensitive to the patient's needs; his attitude reflected understanding, and after ten minutes the young man's anxiety and apprehension subsided.

I accompanied Dr. Burton-Bradley to court, where he served as an expert witness, testifying about a young man accused of rape. Even in the tropics, the presiding judge was dressed in the manner of English judges, wearing judicial robes and a wig. Dr. Burton-Bradley, who was well known by the court, presented his testimony in clear, non-technical terms. The cross-examination was brief, since little of his testimony was questioned.

Dr. Burton-Bradley has served as consultant to many agencies, in addition to being director of the Laloki Mental Hospital, the only psychiatric hospital in New Guinea. He also has consulted with several psychiatric services in scattered parts of the country, visiting these hospitals at regular intervals and in between being available for consultation by short-wave radio. He has managed to find time for individual psychotherapy, not wanting to lose direct patient contact.

Life in the tropics presents many challenges, one of them being the struggle against lassitude. Although many persons coming to the area have surrendered to its temptations, Dr. Burton-Bradley has not. Besides his clinical and administrative duties, he has maintained a substantial interest in research, especially focused on the sudden impact of western patterns on a stone age culture, an impact which is producing rapid social changes with attendant emotional repercusions. His literary output is remarkable.

He has published more than eighty scientific articles and research manuals, and he has contributed to various books, including a new encyclopedia of Papua New Guinea.

Dr. Burton-Bradley displays a sensitive and perceptive approach in his writings, whether he is dealing with the psychiatric disturbance of running amok or with the emotional adjustment of mixed racial groups of New Guinea. He wrote the first psychiatric study of the cargo cult movement and of the emotional state of its leaders, a study significant not only for New Guinea but also for mass movements in other cultures.

Most cultural research done by anthropologists, psychiatrists, and other professionals has been based on field trips of a few weeks to one or two years. Dr. Burton-Bradley, however, has had the unique opportunity of living in the country for more than fifteen years. His experiences not only made him aware of specific aspects of behavior but also resulted in an understanding of the totality of local existence. Having arrived in New Guinea in 1959, he lived there when some parts, particularly the Highlands, were still culturally isolated. Having become part of the country, he became sensitive to and aware of its large problems. As a result, he was able to avoid the dilemma of either forcing foreign standards on another culture or indulging in the unrealistic sentimentality which appears in some of the professional writings on New Guinea.

Dr. Burton-Bradley has contributed greatly to a better understanding of a culture that had remained obscure until recent years, and by so doing he has helped us gain a better understanding of our own culture.

Otto Billig, M.D.
Clinical Professor of Psychiatry
Vanderbilt University

Nashville, Tennessee
October 1974

IN PREPARING the Abraham Flexner lectures for 1973, compiled in this volume, Dr. Burton G. Burton-Bradley drew upon his experiences of living, working, and studying in Papua New Guinea for fifteen years. The information he gathered was unique. He was not only the first psychiatrist but also for most of that time the only psychiatrist serving a population of two-and-a-half million persons, predominantly nonliterate.

In his first lecture, "Stone Age to Twentieth Century," Dr. Burton-Bradley functions as an observer of the larger scene. In sketching a picture of primitive people coming more and more under the influence of outside ideas and pressures, he provides us with a backdrop for the more specific discussions that follow. Of these topics, suicide is an ubiquitous problem. Cargo cult and mixed race marginality are more distinctive, but each has features relevant to other cultures, including our own.

In all of the lectures there is a blending of Dr. Burton-Bradley's rich background knowledge as he draws on his experience in anthropology, public health, general medicine, and psychiatry. This broadness of scope provides a multidimensional view of the problems and of some of the solutions.

Dr. Burton-Bradley has been a pioneer in exploring the psychiatrically uncharted reaches of a remote land. In doing so, he has made one of the most significant contributions to the new and rapidly developing field of transcultural psychiatry. For those who look for a blend of science and adventure, this volume should make interesting and informative reading.

Marc H. Hollender, M.D.
Chairman, Department of Psychiatry
Vanderbilt University

Nashville, Tennessee
October, 1974

Stone Age Crisis

1 Stone Age to Twentieth Century

THE WESTERN component of Oceania, that vast multitude of archipelagoes and islands of the great Pacific Ocean, is known as Melanesia. To the north of this region lies Micronesia, and to the east the scattered groups of Polynesia spread out into the otherwise great emptiness of the mid-Pacific. To the west is Indonesia and to the south the continent of Australia. All these surrounding areas have their impact upon that part of Melanesia which is the subject of the present discussion and which is now known as Papua New Guinea. The linguistic, cultural, economic, and physical features of these countries shade into one another in such a way as to suggest a complex pattern of migration and settlement for the whole region. In addition to this a considerable portion still remains under control of the three alien powers England, France, and Indonesia.

For thousands of years the country has provided an area of refuge for so-called primitive man, with apparently little response from more developed peoples. Why is this so? Although aesthetically attractive in many areas, it is not particularly enticing from the physical point of view. The coasts are often bordered by wide swamps, with much of the mainland covered by dense forest. The interior is characterized by an enormous central cordillera rising to over sixteen thousand feet and more than fifteen hundred miles long extending from one end of the island to the other. With the exception of a number of low-lying coral islands including the Trobriands, many of the other islands are also mountainous. Abundant rainfall in some areas promotes erosion and reduces fertility of the soil. The Gulf District of Papua is probably the wettest land area in the world. Other parts are so parched that famine is a recurring theme. There are few roads outside the principal towns, so that travel is of necessity by aircraft or on foot. Severe earthquakes occur from time to time, and more than a dozen volcanoes exist which occasionally burst into violent activity. In the Gazelle Peninsula of New Britain, the minor earthquake, or *guria*, is a daily event, and in the Central District, the taipan, death adder, and Papuan black snakes are highly lethal. In brief, it is doubtful whether there is any other tropical country with quite the same range of hazardous physical circumstances, and it is against this background that the people have to live their lives and carry on their work. Continuity of contact with peoples of European ancestry is of recent origin, dating from the late nineteenth century, when it was confined mainly to coastal areas; contact was made with the Highlands for the first time in the nineteen thirties and with some remote areas only in recent years. Despite these difficult circumstances, the inhabitants are an attractive and enterprising group of people.

This newly developing nation is made up of a mainland and hundreds of smaller islands and is the most thickly inhabited region of Melanesia. It is much poorer economically than Fiji or New Caledonia, but great efforts are being directed toward its development, including a large copper project on the island of Bougainville. The existing political unit is a neophyte, the product of an amalgam, the Australian Territory of Papua and the United Nations Trust Territory of New Guinea. They were governed as one in an administrative union provided for in the United Nations Trusteeship agreement of 1946. The population consists of more than two and a half million Papuans and New Guineans, a variable number of Caucasian Europeans who come and go and who are in the vicinity of some fifty thousand, six thousand persons of mixed ancestry, and a small Chinese group. At present many Europeans are leaving under the Employment Security Scheme, which was designed to cushion the impact of localization policies on the expatriate. The rural people are predominantly nonliterate, and the individual's social orbit consists of, and is often confined to, his cultural-linguistic group, of which there are more than seven hundred. The psychiatrist soon learns the importance of a number of new factors, among which may be included the local concepts of normality and abnormality, custom, language, and a social organization made up of clans, lineages, phratries, moieties, and cognate groups. As far as neurosis and psychosis are concerned, these factors are important aids in effecting accurate diagnoses. They are less important for the diagnosis of psychosomatic disorders, since the required information is obtained by physical examination, but they are highly significant for etiology and symptom formation.

The country is unique among developing peoples in that it has about one quarter of the world's languages, not dialects, and associated with each one there is to a large extent a distinct culture. Each has its own term to deal with psychotic or insane manifestations—for example, *kavakava* in Hanuabada, *mekakare* in Kerema, *awa'awa* in Marshall Lagoon, *veuari* in Kivori Poe, *lungalunga* in Rabaul, and so on. Fortunately there are three linguae francae to ease the burden: Neomelanesian pidgin, Police Motu, and Bahasia Indonesia.

Prior to the advent of Europeans from overseas, the inhabitants corresponded roughly to the tribes of Northern Europe before the Roman Empire and to those of North America in pre-Columbian times. The nation still does not look like a modern industrial state, and quite possibly may never do so, but it is certainly starting to employ the same symbols and technology and all the outward and visible signs of the emerging world culture. It is perhaps too easy to delude ourselves with these similarities and to assume too readily a greatly accelerated rendering of the process of social change which took many centuries to come about in the northern hemisphere.

Nonetheless, few countries in all history have compressed so much modification into such a small space of time as has this country over the past decade. This statement is no mere platitude, and those of us who have had the good fortune to be present during these formative years are fully aware of the impact on the lives of the people. It is not surprising then that the Minister for Foreign Relations (Kiki 1968) in the second autobiography yet to appear sees his own background as that of ten thousand years in a lifetime. Ahuia Ova's reminiscences (Williams 1939), which preceded Kiki's, have an air of relative constancy and immutability about them. The contrast is striking.

In the precontact era there was continuous warfare of all groups against all others who were in geographical contiguity. Although warrior values die hard, the superimposed peace has reduced warfare to a minimum. Older Papuans and New Guineans refer to these earlier periods with ambivalence. On the one hand they are proud of their skills as warriors when younger, while on the other they refer to the virtue of social order and reduction of killing. The sociocultural influence of these former traditions occasionally manifests itself in the behavior of individuals, for example, in cases of amok explosive reactions and other aggressive acts, including violence, which arise from time to time. Even in the case of organic psychosyndromes, despite the primary importance of irritability and the possible asynchronous discharge of a nerve-cell focus when an epileptic kills, examination reveals the mode of thinking in explanation of his conduct to be expressed in cultural themes rather than individual terms. A further consequence of the peace is elaboration of cargo cult activities, to be discussed in a later chapter.

Social change refers to modifications in the social organization of a society or in its pattern of social roles. Some ten to fifteen years ago Papua New Guinea was considered a stationary sort of place. Newcomers were assured that nothing of any real importance ever happened there. More recently two important events have taken place: First, there has been a great influx of overseas capital from the Australian government and private enterprise, and second, the preparation for self-government and independence has had a marked influence on the life patterns of all groups living in the country. In the earlier part of the century, and even as late as ten to fifteen years ago, the inhabitants of the capital, Port Moresby, wore little clothing; their apparel consisted either of *laplaps*—that is, waistcloths—or grass attire. Not so very long ago they made their tools from wood and stone; their houses of palm thatch and timber were prepared with the aid of an adze. Their diet consisted of yams, fish, and sago. Pots made from local clay were used in the barter. Status depended not on birth but on liberality in providing lavish feasts. Those who gave the biggest and best parties were ultimately accepted as headmen of a sort. Intergroup warfare was then common. But the urban dweller of today who lives in the same place is very different in appearance. Shirts, shorts, and miniskirts are common. His house is of European construction, now made of sawn timber and corrugated iron, and the people enjoy the advantages of piped water, electricity, and garbage disposal services. Most have received some schooling. The economy is now based on money, and men earn their living as artisans, public servants, and businessmen. Status nowadays depends on clothing and occupation. The elite are to be observed playing golf with visiting dignitaries. Intergroup warfare has been replaced by the magistrate. The house servant now learns his bushcraft in the Boy Scouts. The stresses and strains to which he is subjected are also much greater.

But do such factors have a specific pathoplastic effect upon mental disorder? Clinical evidence suggests that they do. This is not to deny that they vary in degree and extent among different cultural-linguistic groups and may even at times have an integrating rather than a disintegrating effect. Sociocultural influences operate with and against a background of genetic, physiological, and psychological forces interacting with one another to produce psychiatric disorder. It is clear that the massive assaults of social change on stabilized mainland and island ecosystems do not take place without some secondary effects. The increase in population densities alone, particularly in urban areas, results in much greater frequency of psychologically traumatic interactions. Many people who are virtually foreigners to one another now come together. Developed systems of transportation and communication produce similar effects. Acculturation stresses arising from such contributing factors as conflict of the generations, racial discrimination, anomie, new class differentials, and the effect of changed structures of educational opportunity all color the picture of psychiatric disease processes.

And what of the effects of impending independence? Although 1974 was the agreed upon year, much apprehension remains. Some fear that the Europeans will leave when independence comes, taking all their money, businesses, property, and expertise with them. Some feel that there will be a failure of health, education, and other services and that there will be a breakdown in law and order. Others believe that large houses, automobiles, universal secondary education, prestigious employment, factories for making money, and factories for making munitions are essential prerequisites for independence. Still others believe that all these things will come about automatically. The last possibility that is mentioned is that the extension of education is likely to modify cargo cult type of thinking. There is inevitable conflict between the coastal peoples and those of the Highlands. The former are

outnumbered, and the latter, who are only barely contacted peoples, fear that their lack of educational opportunity will preclude acquisition of top jobs in the new
administration. There will undoubtedly be problems. The
preliminary period of self-government prior to independence is a step in the right direction, allowing time for
resolution of some of these questions. But I have no doubt
that the Papuans and New Guineans are a resourceful and
innovative group of people quite equal to the task.

2 Cargo Cult

ADJUSTMENT CULT activities, wherein a lesser technology encounters a greater one, have been reported from many different parts of the world since remote antiquity. They are referred to under a variety of names—for example, the Messianic Korean Cult in California, the Taiping Rebellion in China, the Mau Mau in Kenya, the Ghost Dance of the Paiute Indians of North America, the Xhosa Cult of South Africa, the movement associated with the so-called Mad Mullah of Somaliland, and many others. Central to them all are disparities of status between markedly different cultures, between subcultures, and between persons, with associated conflict and anxiety and characterized by unproductive rituals. There is, however, a strong wish for resolution of social, economic, and political problems and a desire for a better life. The specifically Melanesian form is known as *cargo cult*, and this form does not occur outside the area. This subvariety receives its local coloring from the following factors: First, there is the intense individualism of the people and the great concern with wealth, both in its customary display and in conspicuous consumption. Second, there is interaction with the spirit world through the agency of hallucinations, a feature uncommon in social movements not of the cargo cult type, and people seek satisfaction in an imaginative projection. Third, the expressions of self-esteem and the modes of achieving manhood are locally devised. For example, one is important by virtue of the number of pigs one has, the number of one's wives, one's fertility, and the size of one's yams. Fourth, there are hundreds of microlinguistic and culturally distinct groups. A cult may be confined to the language area; occasionally it is diffused widely through the use of neomelanesian pidgin. Fifth, there is the concept of cargo which appeared from about 1935 onwards on the mainland of New Guinea as an updated and displaced symbol of traditional wealth. In the time of Virchow, movements of this kind were seen as aberrations, as parallels of mental disorder. Nowadays they are understood as purely social in nature, as collective efforts to solve a common problem. Although understandable in this way, an exclusively social explanation is a partial one only, omitting significant medical and psychological variables. Existing theories based on the social model could be greatly strengthened by the incorporation of findings from these additional sources. Cults are not always constructive by any means, and at times they can make demands beyond the power of some individuals to cope, with decompensation and breakdown of certain ego-defense mechanisms. In addition, people with already existing psychiatric disorders are often attracted to, and rewarded by, prestigious tasks within the system and are thus consolidated in their roles and in their mental disorder. They have the charisma, and they want the job. Cargo thinking is endemic in this country and colors the symptomatology of many psychiatric disorders. Grandiosity and the grandiose delusion are invariably associated with cult behavior. I shall refer to field and clinical evidence in support of an expanded interpretation.

Although there can be considerable variation in detail in different cults, there is a basic nucleus common to most of them. I shall try to present this for convenience in the form of an amalgam. Cargo thinking meets psychological needs. Cult development offers a possible alternative to the economic system introduced from abroad, and it requires a conflict engendered by material interests and differential status to bring it to the surface. A prophet, leader, or messiah emerges. He is often a mediocrity, as measured by different cultural standards, and one who is not averse to the use, or threatened use, of sorcery in bringing dissidents into line, although recourse to this action is seldom necessary. He has a fantasy solution to offer his followers initiated by a revelation which may take the form of a dream or visual hallucination, both powerful agents in effecting conversion. He proclaims a great future event, or a millenium, and may even provide the specific date. Preparations are made to deal with the expected changes. Airstrips, wharves, or helipads are constructed to receive the ancestral spirits who bear the much-valued cargo. An iconoclastic contraculture may develop, and new social mores may be adopted. Money is destroyed, food gardens are neglected, and livestock killed on the theory that they will no longer be needed. When prophecy fails, the cult wanes and becomes latent.

Cargo cult activities have been reported since the late nineteenth century, although, as we have already indicated, they did not then receive this designation. It is highly likely that they have existed in this area since time immemorial, for the circumstances giving rise to them are not solely of recent origin. Technology is that component of culture, including tools and knowledge, that man uses to control his physical environment in order to achieve desired practical ends. There is nothing new in this, and disparate technologies in contact are part of the human condition, have always been so, and are likely to remain so for quite some time to come. In the Annual Report of 1893 the Samarai Magistrate R. J. Kennedy describes a young man named Tokerua who had stated that he was in communication with a spirit who resided in a traditionally sacred tree. This hallucinatory experience was associated with a dissociative reaction, and his face was said to be transfigured. He prophesied a catastrophe in which the whole coast would be submerged in a tidal wave. The people listened to him, abandoned their houses, and built new ones farther inland. They did no work, destroyed three hundred of their pigs, and consumed the remaining food in their gardens. They asserted that these items were no longer needed now that Tokerua was in charge. His followers eventually became disillusioned with him.

F. E. Williams, the government anthropologist for Papua, spent twenty years in field work in the course of which he endeavored to see and evaluate the operation of psychological factors in the motives and ideals of the people. He saw the individual as selective in response to the cultural impact, and he was fully aware of the dehumanizing effect of those generalizations which view the particular human being as an abstraction. His account of the Vailala Madness (Williams 1923, 1934) was the first systematic study of what was eventually to be categorized as cargo cult. In this there was much evidence of psychological contagion and mass hysteria. He stressed the importance of the leader whose behavior could be looked upon as the product of motivational impulses, specific cognitive media available to the individual, and values of the alien culture. He described a group of people from different villages, whom he described as *automaniacs* and who acknowledged one man as leader. There was mutual adaptation of the psychopathology of individuals; they balanced each other, and this allowed the group to function as it did for at least a decade. Even to this day fragments or *formes frustes* from this area still make their appearance in the symptomatology of psychiatric patients. The cult of this area is now passive and latent, but the potentialities remain.

Since the time of Kennedy and Williams, the vast majority of investigations into cargo cult have been made by cultural anthropologists, who are the pioneers in this field. I cannot discuss these here, and I refer you to the bibliog-

graphies of Leeson (1952) and Worsley (1968). Detailed ethnographies of particular areas have been produced by
Burridge (1960) on the Bogia region, by Maher (1961) in
relation to the Tommy Kabu movement in the Purari delta,
by Schwartz (1962) on the Paliau movement in the Manus
District, and by Lawrence (1964) on Yali, who became the
outstanding cargo cult leader of the Rai Coast. Wideranging comparative studies are few in number. They have
been done mostly by nonresidents with limited access to
the material, and their data are inevitably second-hand. In
addition, psychiatrists, psychologists, and physicians
have in the past shown little interest in the phenomenon.

Dreams and hallucinations are prominent events in the
precipitation of cults and are a common feature in the
symptomatology of those patients in whom cargo thinking
is predominant. The dreams of the nonliterate person are
of cardinal importance to the examining physician and
should compel his rigorous attention. There is a grade of
reality attributable to the explicit manifest content of the
dream that has little or no correlate in the mind of the
sophisticated observer, for the physical and spiritual
worlds are seen as two different phases of the same thing.
What happens in the dream has a reality like that of the
external world. If someone treats you unfairly in a dream,
you might be obliged to take action against the person
concerned in real life, according to customary law, and this
has led to acts of violence and homicide. There is need to
recognize the place of spirits and spirits' adventures
(dreams) in the cosmic order and the significance of all this
in the prediction of individual acts of behavior. All patients should be asked about their dreams, and a detailed
history of any dream volunteered is most desirable. This
should be done irrespective of whether the account should
subsequently be proved factual, overelaborated, or merely
a figment, for its importance as a life-saving measure at
times should never be forgotten.

Cargo cult leaders are of three main kinds: the prophet, the messiah, and the practically motivated leader. They are for the most part discrete entities, but the types can at times overlap one another in practice. The prophet is the one who initiates a cult through a dream or hallucination, and the messiah is believed to be able to bring the cargo millennium to pass. The practically motivated leader endeavors to guide the cult or movement in a workable direction which he considers to be the best. Well-defined disease entities have appeared among them, including schizophrenia, affective psychosis, paranoia, *folie à deux*, epilepsy, hysteria, chronic syphilitic meningoencephalitis, and thyrotoxic psychosis (Burton-Bradley 1970). Three deputies had personalities consistent with sociopathy, as this term is defined in standard textbooks, even when considered against the background of their indigenous social contexts. An interesting account of the leader and deputy in the Yangoru Cargo Cult of 1971 is contained in Hwekmarin, Jamenan, and Lea (1971). The leader is described as a recluse who locks himself in his house for long periods, and the deputy is stated to have been involved in frequent fighting and in trouble with the police and to suffer from epilepsy.

The idea that important social change can be effected by the efforts of individual leaders has been unpopular over the last generation, because of a general distaste for exaggerated hero worship, and what has become known as "the great man hypothesis of historical causation" has had its greatest opponent in White (1949). More recently White's view is losing ground, largely as the result of the studies of Hook (1955) and L'Etang (1969). The work of these authors, while not denying the contributions of other factors, clearly indicates the crucial importance of the dominant individual. Certainly, as far as the cargo cult leader is concerned, many officials and kinsmen would be happier if he were healthier than he often is, and it is undesirable that his illness should catalyze explosive situations to his own detriment and to that of the many who come under his influence.

Cargo anxiety is the essential feature of many instances of pathological anxiety in Melanesia. It is essentially a status anxiety which arises from imbalance between the forces making for development and those of the status quo. It is the consequence of cultural encounter. It permeates almost all aspects of group life, often in covert or subdued form, and it embellishes the symptomatology of many forms of psychiatric disorder. Let us look at some cases that I have examined in hospital and field situations. Each patient is a real or potential cargo leader, fortuitously cut short in the course of his career.

In one instance a twenty-five-year-old male from Bougainville was admitted to hospital with a history of violent behavior in his village. He had fought those who opposed his beliefs. He exhibited the cardinal signs of anxiety, yet assumed a grandiose attitude toward staff and patients. He stated that he had been sent by God to free all the patients in hospital, and he told them to destroy their vegetable gardens, as they would have no further use for them. Following high doses of chlorpromazine, his aggressive and restless behavior subsided and he was subsequently discharged from the hospital. There was a genetic history of mental illness. A visit to his village revealed that he was the ringleader in the faction against the antimalaria spraying program, which was contrary to his cargo beliefs and was in his view unnecessary. There were those who were for him, those who sat on the fence, and those who were against him. The last group called him *longlong*. This term formerly referred to one who was either insane, confused, or suffering from some serious form of physical disability. Today it appears to have crystallized into a narrower meaning, referring to the obligatory nonconformist, that is, the one who suffers from mental disorder.

This man was married, with six children. He said that he was too important to work, but investigation showed that he had been a mission catechist and was educated to Standard 5. He said that he was preparing for the millennium and had designed a flag which would be accepted in his area first and later throughout the world. This flag would stop all hate and all war and revolutionize the economy with plentiful cargo for everyone. It contained three stars representing Father, Son, and Holy Spirit, had a human figure at the base (the Virgin Mary), and a tree with ten twigs (the Ten Commandments). He suspected that he was the subject of sorcery by an unknown person, and this was delaying the achievement of his objectives.

A young male indigene in his mid-twenties came from the Northern District of Papua. The older people of the village claim that he had a normal upbringing as a child. He was still being breast-fed when the Japanese invaded in the Second World War. He and his parents spent six months in the jungle during this time under very difficult circumstances. Both he and the village people stated that his father suffered from a mental illness. The father would get up in the middle of the night and light a fire to dry rubber. Local Orokaivans insist that such behavior is not normal for their people. While he was working in Port Moresby his European supervisor introduced a new method of work to reduce wastage. He did not co-operate in the change and was told that he would be dismissed on that account. He then attacked the supervisor and bit him on the buttock. He would not release the bite until another employee forced a stick between his teeth. It was about this time that the spirit of his dead grandfather appeared before him and told him to go home and look after the village cemetery. This he did. Then he commenced to dig a deep hole in a certain place. He said that in due course he would come to a big snake with the skin like a white man and that the snake would lead him to paradise. While there he would find a thousand dollars. The hole ended up about twenty feet deep. While digging, he received the daily moral support of a bird who pressed him to continue digging. At various times during the course of the digging he exhibited a certain vagueness, would not look people directly in the eyes, and would place his hands on his genitalia while talking. Cargo cult beliefs were widespread among the people of this area, who had formerly experienced the Baigona and Taro cults. Just before the Japanese came to Buna in 1942, cargo cult activities developed in this area and again in 1943 at Tufi after the Japanese landed. The people stopped working, killed pigs and dogs, and spent a lot of time dancing. They said the whole world was turning over with the Europeans fighting. There is no doubt that during the earlier period of this man's digging he had a strong following; as the digging failed to produce results, followers began to fall away or suspend judgment, but never at any time was he without followers. Even later, when he was confined to a mental hospital, his escape from that institution was financed by his own *wantoks* in Port Moresby in order that they might assist him to return home some fifty miles and continue the digging. With the passage of time, taunts began to increase. One woman laughed at him many times. He then concealed himself in the *kunai* grass near the roadside and confronted the woman as she passed by. He threw a spear into her thorax and killed her by cutting her five times with an axe. He ran to the adjacent village where he was seen, covered in blood, to throw a spear at another girl, and he attempted to cut an old woman before he was overpowered. The event had all the characteristics of an *amok* response. One observer stated that he wore army clothes at the time. When arrested he was dressed in his brother's army uniform, a Japanese steel helmet decorated with photographs of himself, feathers, and various pieces of red cloth designed to represent sergeant's sashes and garter tabs. He wore three pairs of socks at once. He was convicted of murder and referred for psychiatric assessment. Examination revealed vagueness, thought disorder, marked affective incongruity, a history of heredofamilial mental illness, and grandiosity. None of the followers shared his beliefs with the same fixity and unchanging intensity. He had dug the hole for three years. He was suffering from paranoid schizophrenia.

A single male indigene from the Western District of Papua in his mid-thirties was brought to hospital after haranguing a group of followers. When examined he claimed to be in communication with President Johnson of the United States through the aid of a walkie-talkie. He demonstrated the manner in which he did this, showing that the source of the ideas was his earlier service with the armed forces. He had told the people to demonstrate pro-American sentiments, otherwise he would insure that American planes would punish any anti-American-thinking people. Those who showed their allegiance would be well rewarded with unlimited bounty. He stated that his close association with President Johnson was because he (himself) was a Christlike person who could co-opt any of the major political powers to bring about desired ends. Serological evidence pointed to the existence of general paresis. The Wassermann reaction was strongly positive in tests of both blood and cerebrospinal fluid. The colloidal gold curve was of the paretic type. He received a total of twenty million units of penicillin and became less expansive. His beliefs did not entirely disappear, but they became less florid. A social remission ensured and he was discharged from hospital. Twelve months later I saw him addressing a large crowd and at the same time talking into a mouthpiece of a public telephone, claiming again to be in communication with President Johnson. He was apprehended on suspicion of mental disorder and brought again for examination. His grandiose delusions, which were considerably reduced some twelve months before, were now again more in evidence and had assumed a dominant role. They gradually subsided with hospitalization and treatment. His superficial sophistication and knowledge of technology derived from army service had left a strong impression upon his followers, who were still inquiring after him some five years later.

A young indigene from the Marobe District of New Guinea was aged twenty-two years when first admitted to hospital in 1965. There was a family history of hypomanic personality. He was hyperactive and overtalkative and exhibited flight of ideas. He said that he was going to marry a European nursing sister, and he seemed not greatly perturbed by her rejection of him. He claimed to be going to America in order to have his skin changed to white, declaring that he would provide the passage money by growing a patch of *kau kau* (sweet potato). He could do all this easily, he said, because he was Jesus Christ. While in the village he heard the voice of God, who told him to go first to Australia and then to America, thus insuring the future well-being of his own village *wantoks*. The manic phase gradually subsided when he was given a total dosage of 800 mg of chlorpromazine each day for one week. He was then friendly but still slightly hypomanic. His grandiose delusional system was still in evidence, and he still claimed that he would marry the European nursing sister and go to America, but these beliefs did not then occupy such a central position in his ideation. He saw no incongruity in his intention to finance the trip to America and preparing for it by planting a bed of *kau kau*. He had a large following both in the town and the village. His lack of success in coping with an urban environment was responsible for the decision to repatriate him to his home village. He was not heard of again until four years later, when another manic episode necessitated his readmission to hospital. His *wantoks* were again very much in evidence. Their enthusiasm was quite out of proportion to that usually shown under such circumstances. His manic charm and claim to special preternatural capacity had clearly left its mark upon them.

In another case, a man suffering from the preictal irritability of grand-mal epilepsy prophesied the end of the world, giving the day, month, and year; he said that an earthquake would deliver ancestors from below laden with cargo, so that work and school would be no longer necessary. Such was the extent of his charisma that property and money were destroyed by others who had fully identified with his beliefs.

A public servant from the Morobe District, who was suffering from schizophrenia, isolated himself and built a house on the periphery of the village. He constructed a high fence to prevent others from entering. He then killed his child by smashing its head against a rock, saying that the baby was blocking the road to cargo. After the infant's death, the man said that he would go to Port Moresby to obtain a white baby, after which an abundance of cargo would arrive. Such a retiring person is unlikely to become a cargo leader by himself but is excellent material for the efficient deputy working in an explosive cargo atmosphere.

A middle-aged man from the Milne Bay District, who suffered from narcolepsy and tuberculous spondylitis, was referred for treatment by the court. He had been found guilty of murdering his child. This concerned him less than the gonorrhea that he had contracted and which had led to much gossip in his village and a state of uneasiness and chronic anxiety. A lowly status stemming from biological and aesthetic inferiority was further reduced by this circumstance. A psychotic solution was virtually inevitable. He heard a voice saying that the Queen wanted him to visit Australia and that the District Commissioner had put him in charge of his area to insure a new era of plenty for all. He would shout at an imaginery audience, saying that he was "King of the World" and that plenty of cargo would come. Hospitalization prevented the occurrence of any further cargo development.

An elderly man from the Gulf District was referred by the local doctor for treatment of a suspected paranoid condition. The patient's relatives and friends felt that his mental state had deteriorated over the previous three years. Their reasons were based on his glaring ignorance of business principles. He had had a trade store for ten years. Three years before he had built a much larger store adjoining the original one, which he had stocked with goods but had never opened, with the result that the condition of much of the stock had deteriorated, and a debt of seventeen thousand dollars had been built up. The creditors reached the point where they were exercising their right to recoup their losses. He was well known as a strong believer in cargo cult, but he lacked a following in his area. A further source of serious concern was his recent purchase of a shotgun, an action out of keeping with the rest of his character. The authorities in the area received meaningless accounts from him on numerous occasions, indicative of thought disorder, as well as calculations referring to shares in his business amounting to over a million dollars. Several of his communications were signed "Prime Minister" and "District Commissioner." He had also dreamed that he could ascend into heaven on a ladder from his store. A provisional diagnosis of paranoid schizophrenia was made.

Of special interest is the reversible grandiose paranoid reaction occurring in the young man without a following but liberally endowed with cargo ideology. He asserts or implies that he is Jesus Christ or some other prestigious figure and is referred to the psychiatrist for treatment. This disorder needs careful distinction from the purely natural aspirations of the immature and youthful person. The evidence of gross distortion of reality defined as such by the alien medical examiner (heteropathology) and the patient's own kinsmen (autopathology) will usually clarify the issue. The reaction is usually of short duration and is analogous to the persecutory paranoid reaction characteristic of technologically developed societies. The young man is a person who has not yet experienced some of the acephalous mass hysterias which abound in an atmosphere of cargo wants and psychological contagion. Should he ever do so, he runs the risk of reinforcing his disorder and precipitating a cult. Let us look at two such cases.

A thirty-three-year-old man from Manus Island was referred for treatment by the court following threatening behavior towards a storekeeper. He claimed that a staff member had refused to give him five hundred dollars from his twenty-million-dollar bank account, that he owned Ansett Airlines and an 8,000-ton cargo ship which was in the harbor at the time. He stated that many people were jealous of him and his wealth, that he would take to court any person who frustrated him, and that he was going to establish a new order, repair the wartime airstrip, and build a national airline to be known as the Million Line. In this way he would be ready for the cargo that was sure to come. Treatment with psychotropic drugs and rehabilitation therapy were followed by a full remission in his condition three weeks later.

A twenty-one-year-old overweight male from Marshall Lagoon was admitted to hospital in a manic state. He said that he had been appointed by God to lead Papua New Guinea. He had given up his education because it was boring. There were more important things to do. He heard the voice of God saying that he was to be Prime Minister to insure an era of plenty of cargo and well-being for all. Initially he would be leader of the Opposition. The present holder of that office was a good man, he said, but did not have enough skill to defeat the Government. He appointed another patient as his deputy. His parents had had high expectations of achievement and had overindulged the growing boy with excess food. This plus a deformity from a childhood injury and failure to meet academic expectations precipitated a compensatory grandiosity, the content of which followed standard cargo lines. Rest and psychotropic drug therapy were followed by a full remission in his condition one month later.

Cargo cult followers, as individuals, may go through a series of pro-cult, anti-cult, non-cult, or fence-sitter phases at various stages of their existence. The more immediate followers surrounding the leader, who might well be called his praetorian guard, include among their members people suffering from hysteria, psychopathy, and at times epilepsy. The vast majority of followers prior to and subsequent to overt cult manifestations are almost certainly in a state of good mental health. The precise position could only be established by direct clinical examination of all the people involved—an impractical procedure, for the distribution of cargo beliefs is wide indeed. Some say the prophet is a wise man, others that he is *longlong* and liable to cause trouble with the Government; others are not interested, and still others say that they will wait and see. Clearly we have to consider the possibility of the healthy person in the sick group, if it can be categorized as such at times, as well as the sick person in the sick group. Their mutual psychopathologies balance and compensate each other to sustain the system. On the whole, however, I would doubt the utility of labeling large sections of a population running into many thousands as mentally unhealthy, or on the other hand as healthier than unbelieving neighbors. Each individual has to be assessed on his merits by the criteria of scientific medicine. There remains the problem that all destructive group behavior, whether criminal or psychotic, must be opposed. The extent to which these behaviors are based upon want of self-esteem resulting from social injustice, or from other causes and combinations of causes, has to be appraised and rectified. At times the leader, with the active support of many followers and the enthusiastic acquiescence of most, has succeeded in leading a cultural-linguistic group to widespread destructive activities through the perversion of essentially rational political institutions.

I now refer to three instances of human sacrifice related to cargo cult activities with which I have been closely associated and whose principals have come under my care. Discussions with well-informed persons lead me to suspect that the practice is, or has been, more widespread than is generally believed. In Papua New Guinea, information on the causes of death is inevitably second or third hand in many cases, so that the true incidence is unknown. Two of the sacrificers suffered from grandiose paranoia, the third from paranoid schizophrenia. The first two had attracted followers; all three had made attempts to speed up the arrival of cargo through emulation of the Christian Passion. The importance of careful history taking is obvious. When a cultist tells you that he is going to kill himself or someone else, it is wise to take him seriously. This can be important at any time, but is particularly so when a decision has to be made either to admit a person to hospital or discharge him.

In the first case, an elderly male *luluai* from the Madang District was admitted to hospital after killing a friend. The two men had discussed for years ways and means of raising their status to that of industrialized peoples with all their material appurtenances. The *luluai*, who was also a mission catechist, decided the only way to do this was to emulate the Christian Passion, on the assumption that the advent of Christianity was responsible for the wealth and standing of the Europeans. His friend readily agreed that this was so. He arranged the erection of an enclosure in the

village with a platform in the centre from which he addres-
sed his followers. He invited the Bishop to a ceremony, the
nature and purpose of which he did not reveal. He then
obtained a long American bush knife, took his friend by
the hand, and led him into the enclosure. All those present
later insisted that the friend was fully co-operative. The
friend than raised his hand to "the sun, the moon, and the
stars" to inform these cosmic forces of what was about to
be done. The friend then put his head back, offering his
neck, and the *luluai* made one quick violent blow with the
knife. Blood flowed freely; the friend fell to the ground and
died. Most of those present ran away. In explanation later,
the *luluai* stated that some years previously the friend
asserted that the spirit of God had appeared before him
and said he must die and shed blood as did Jesus Christ to
insure a wonderful series of changes in the lives of the
people. These included a new ethical system in which
there would be no more fighting, no more stealing of pigs,
no more quarrels over women, and a new era of prestige
and material goods.

According to the McNaghten Rules, to avoid assignment
of responsibility a defendent must show that he was labor-
ing under such a defect of reason from disease of the mind
as not to know the nature and quality of the act or, if he did
know it, that he did not know he was doing what was
wrong. In Papua New Guinea, the Queensland Criminal
Code has been adopted. The law relating to the excusatory
effect of insanity under this code follows, but also
goes beyond, the common-law rules formulated in
McNaghten's case. Wrongfulness is interpreted to mean
"wrong, having regard to the everyday standards of
reasonable people." For the rural villager, the reasonable
people who make up his particular world are his own
wantoks; for the urbanized individual, the reasonable people are not only his *wantoks*, but the rest of the community
as well. In addition, this code adds a further ground of

excuse, namely, if the mental disease results in depriving the sufferer of the capacity to control his actions. At the trial, the *luluai* was found guilty but insane at the time of committing the crime. He was ordered to be kept at Her Majesty's pleasure in the Corrective Institution. He was later transferred to the now defunct Bomana Mental Hospital and subsequently to the Laloki Psychiatric Center. It was clear that his belief fulfilled the three essential technical criteria of delusion. First, he had a belief that was in fact false. Second, it was one completely impervious and unshakable to reasoning and argument. Third, it was not held in the same persistent way by the people of his own cultural-linguistic group, that is, his kinsmen. They said they did not hold the belief and would only accept it if they could see the wonderful changes take place with their own eyes. The belief pattern was rapidly abandoned by those of his followers who had seemed to hold it earlier on. The *luluai*, however, remained firm, and when examined many months later he still held the same belief along with many other fantasies. The symptom pattern was consistent with grandiose paranoia. The friend's visual hallucination and co-operation in his own death make it probable that he too had the same beliefs as the *luluai*. He certainly was the passive entity in a setting of what the French call *folie à deux*, or the madness of two.

In a second case an elderly man from the Bougainville District was committed for trial on a charge of willful murder. At the termination of the preliminary hearing he attempted to cut his throat. He made two further attempts at a later stage. He was not depressed, the acts were no mere hysterical gestures, and the threat to his own life was quite real in each instance. In explanation he stated that he was uninterested in the proceedings and would enter the other world to return later. And he continued to commute between the two worlds with all the precision of a yo-yo. He had killed his grand-nephew. He took him behind a village house and cut him on the back of the neck with a large bush knife, an act when fell just short of complete decapitation. The head was still attached by a flap of skin at the front of the neck. By this action, he said, he became God, and as a result much cargo in the form of motor cars, houses, food, transistor radios, and other goods would arrive by ship and aircraft. For five years other villagers considered that he had changed in character and was in a state of permanent anxiety. The delusional state was not present in the other villagers, but it was still present in the defendant some twelve months later.

In another case of similar nature, a young man charged with murder had read about Jesus fasting and about Abraham considering the sacrifice of his son Isaac. For eight days he ate nothing, controlling his hunger by swallowing the saliva from his betel-nut chew. He then took his small infant son into the bush and cut his heart out, chopped it up into small pieces, ate a little of it, and then cooked the rest with some glue, so that the smoke would, as he said, go up to heaven. By so doing he hoped to bring great wealth to his own people. He was a withdrawn type of person who had suffered paternal deprivation at an early period of life. Although the provision of a substitute father tends to compensate for this in the closely knit traditional society, it did not do so in his case. He lacked a decisive interpersonal relationship of the type essential for proper maturation. He was trying to emulate component aspects of some teachings of Christian literature in order to better the lives of those around him. He misinterpreted the intent of those teachings, but correctly assessed their content and literal meaning. Given the limited psychological orbit in which he operated, it might at first appear that his thinking was normal within this framework. The bizarre quality of the act, however, with its morbid mutilating aspects, the family history of mental illness, the beliefs concerning the sacrifice of his own child which were not held by his own kinsmen, and the threshold-lowering effect in a predisposed person of the inevitable changes in body chemistry consequent upon acute starvation with its ketosis and breakdown in electrolyte homeostasis, clearly put the case in the area of abnormality, that is, paranoid schizophrenia.

Durkheim, in his influential book on suicide, (Durkheim 1897) was endeavoring to combat the extensive psychologism of his day, and in so doing he was led to maintain an exclusive significance for social factors, with unfortunate consequences. For half a century the fetish for disciplinary purity has led, by and large, to the analysis of group phenomena by methods which exclude the techniques and findings of psychiatry. Today, however, the position is slowly changing. We no longer attempt the psychologizing of social analysis, but recognize a synthesis whereby all institutional arrangements are seen as being ultimately channeled through the conduct of individuals, both normal and abnormal. This is not the reduction of one discipline to another, but the union of two for a comprehensive psychosocial analysis. The interdisciplinary approach of transcultural psychiatry has something to offer not only in theory and meaning of cargo cult, but also in the medical and psychiatric treatment of those cult members who are suffering from disease. I postulate a theory of cargo cult based on status anxiety. All thinkers whom I have examined, whether leaders, followers, or members in any other role within the system, see their positions vis-à-vis others, both within the group and outside of it, in a light that fails to please them. All have a common goal in the correction of this deficiency. What determines the emergence of leadership among these people? Clearly, the leader is one who is different from the others in that he claims to have the technique, or others claim that he has, to deliver the real or symbolic cargo within a reasonable time, and all that this implies. The attitudes and beliefs of potential followers will vary but will be influenced by their desires and aspirations within the framework of the psychological and social orbit in which they operate and of which they have knowledge. The leader must meet these needs. He must be a special kind of person. This restricts the range of candidates, and it is not surprising that recruitment of mentally disordered or marginal individuals to cult leadership serves the purpose. Historical, religious, economic, and other contextual factors interact with one another and play their part in determining the form a given cult will tend to take. But behavior in the long run stems from individuals. I contend that medical and psychological variables have been largely ignored in previous rational theories of explanation, to the detriment of a fuller understanding of the phenomenon. In the process cultists have been unwittingly denied access to treatment by virtue of this fact.

It is the basic right of all human beings to accept or reject medical treatment as they so wish, with the possible exception of the psychotic person who is a danger to himself or others. It should also be their right to know that treatment is available to which they may have easy access. These matters are fully provided for in the Mental Disorders and Treatment Ordinance (1960) and the Native Customs (Recognition) Ordinance (1963). Diagnosis must be based on objective criteria, not on value judgments. Does the patient transgress the norms of his own culture, as so defined by knowledgeable kinsmen? And if so, is the transgression in accord with standard nosological entities of scientific medicine? Clearly we have to face the fact of the possibility of sick persons occupying important roles in the future.

What can be said concerning the future of cargo cult behavior and the recruitment of sick individuals to various functions within the system? Rapid social change is taking place under the influence of economic growth, educational opportunities, and the effect of European values in relation to material appurtenances. But some cultural elements are more refractory to change than others. I think it can be said that cargo cult is unlikely to disappear overnight, nor as readily as some might expect. It will certainly undergo modification. Naïve check forging among schizoid personalities is one instance; healthy forms of productive economic activity is another. Psychiatric treatment is desirable where indicated. An expanding economy should have a favorable effect on status disparities and their inevitable psychological consequences. However, it is well to remember that cultists have no monopoly on institutionalized irrationality. We have only to look at some of the massive parallels in technologically developed societies and the methods employed in coping with them.

3 Suicide

ATTEMPTS TO determine the incidence and prevalence of suicidal acts and other forms of suicidal behavior in lately contacted and technologically underdeveloped Papua New Guinea are fraught with difficulty. Even in developed countries there is often doubt concerning what constitutes a case, and uncritical reliance on official statistics and on the value systems and status of the observer is always unwarranted.

Following some preliminary attempts at definition which laid insufficient emphasis on volition, Durkheim (1952) arrived at the following. He applied the term *suicide* to all cases of death resulting directly or indirectly by a positive or negative act of the victim himself which he knows will produce this result. But in a country like Papua New Guinea, who knows who really wants to die? Does the subject always know? Does the observer always know? In any individual case who knows who actually committed the fatal act? How can the observable and reported data be related to the motivational component of Durkheim's definition, that is, who was the prime mover in the events, and to what end were the actions directed? For those of us who have traveled often down the labyrinthine forensic pathway from *mens rea* to *actus reus* these are significant questions for which the answers are not readily available.

In addition to the problem of definition, available information on the death of an individual is inevitably second hand and suspect. Limited reliance can be placed on the impartiality and the accuracy of data supplied by traders, ubiquitous raconteurs, some missionaries, and many other informants. Even the scientifically trained are frequently the unconscious victims of their own language and value systems. The process of lining village people employed by officers in the field, however admirable in obtaining data for other purposes, is more appropriate to the parade ground and not particularly impressive as a technique in defining and diagnosing cases of suicide. In the developing country suicide is a subject, not unlike alcoholism, on which many people give voice to firm opinions which service their own underlying needs and which could hardly be described as scientific appraisals of the facts. On the one hand, an alien observer might feel that the incidence ought to bear some relationship to that of his own culture, rationalizing this in terms of general principles; and on the other, the indigenous observer with genuine pride in his own country might feel that such an assessment is incorrect and tend to underrate the true situation. How does one count the intrapsychic units of cognition implicit in Durkheim's definition? What reliance can be placed on the extrapsychic units of alleged behavior as reported by different informants? How does one establish the nexus between intrapsychic and extrapsychic unit?

Here are some further practical questions confronting the medical epidemiologist. Who observes what? What are the criteria for making an accurate diagnosis of suicide in predominantly nonliterate Papua New Guinea by the survey methods that are available? Could one be satisfied with these criteria, or could one make do with an educated guess? Does one mean by observation, direct observation of the facts, or the claimed observations of others as reported to one or to one's coworkers on, say, six monthly visits to remote outstations? Who views the bodies? How many of those who die will be seen by a qualified medical practitioner before death? Does he, or does the medical epidemiologist live with the people on the spot in the same way as the anthropologist does, and if so, for how long? How is the linguistic problem handled in a country of some seven hundred different languages? To what extent is a lingua franca appropriate to the jungle context in which the observer operates, as far as the diagnosis of suicide is concerned? If, as seems likely, he deals with evidential rather than experimental data, does he insist upon the rules of evidence of the kind used in a court of law as being the only ones whereby a case can honestly be established as one of suicide? If he is successful in surmounting these difficulties, how does he cope with the nonlinguistic component of communication? In some areas indigenous custom does not allow individuals to speak their own names, or the names of some others, including those who have attempted or committed suicide. Even in those regions where this is not proscribed by custom some people fear that the giving of information will lead to acts of sorcery. Adoptions of children by different parents, and different spellings of the same name will lead to the recording of false data. What can be done about all this?

In view of the fact that fabrication and related activities are known to be part of the business of accommodation and adaptation of the indigenous person in the culture contact-conflict situation, and do not always have the same quasi-ethical connotations to which the white medical practitioner and epidemiologist have been accustomed, what action should be taken to eliminate these factors in the assessment of a case of suicide? From what methodological base does the investigator operate? Does he take due account of the findings of psychiatry, cultural anthropology, and law without which his putative suicidal data would be largely defective? Does he accept Durkheim's view that the suicide rate is culture-specific, with different rates for different cultures, and does he take this into account in relating isolated samples to a universe of hundreds of distinct cultures? Are his assistants instructed on these matters, and do they seek expert help in these fields? What controls are used? What evaluations and corroborations from independent observers are employed?

With these considerations in mind, it is to be noted that nine indigenous deaths were officially reported and categorized as suicide during the year 1969 and eight during 1970. It can be inferred that, given the nature and terrain of the country with its difficulties of transport and communication at all levels, and the problems as already indicated, this figure is undoubtedly an underestimation of the totality. The value of such cases lies in their clinical description, their cultural content, and their relationship to social change. Also, I reported and categorized as suicide during the five-year period from January 1961 to December 1965 forty-one cases for the whole country, a similar reportage rate of 0.7 per 100,000 (Parker and Burton-Bradley 1966). On the other hand, Stanhope (1966) noted five suicides in 58,480 person-years of observation in five rural populations, giving an annual rate of 8.5 per 100,000 in those areas, and Scragg (1966) five suicides in 20,241 person-years of observation in a New Ireland population of 16,600, giving an annual rate of 30 per 100,000 for that area. These last two are interesting observations, noted incidentally in the course of other investigations. Hoskin, Friedman, and Cawte (1969) claim a high incidence in the Kandrian Subdistrict of West New Britain.

None of these studies has made any great inroads into the problems of definition and diagnosis. What is required in each case is the recognition and application of those categories that are relevant to a psychiatric verdict of suicide and not merely the crude accounting procedures that are employed today. Without a clear conception of the entities involved, epidemiological studies are of limited utility. Statistics are useless if we do not know what we are counting. There is still plenty of room for a qualified approach, however, and direct clinical observation of failed suicides and study of all the known circumstances surrounding individual successful suicides immediately after the event has most to offer at the present time.

The methods of suicide employed are governed by fashionable techniques and beliefs concerning their efficacy. Hanging is most favored and adopted equally by both sexes. Vines, ropes, bandages, and torn bedsheets have been employed for this purpose. Next in importance is derris-root poisoning. Other methods include jumping off a coconut tree or cliff, cutting one's throat with a razor blade or knife, allowing someone else to cut one's throat, shooting oneself, pouring kerosene over oneself and applying a lighted match, running *amok* to insure a fatal retribution, allowing others to kill one as an act of sacrifice for magico-religious purposes, holding a detonator against the abdomen, placing one's head in a fire, taking an overdose of an easily procured antimalarial drug, chloroquin, or other readily available noxious material, for example, battery acid, and after the fashion of classical antiquity, jumping onto the spike of a sharp digging stick. With the exception of magico-religious suicide and the *amok* runner most methods are not associated with long periods of deliberation and reflection.

In the summer of 1961, in response to an inquiry, I endeavored to obtain suicide figures for three subdistricts of the Northern District of Papua. In the absence of recorded data the indigenous councilors were asked to make a list of suicides known to them in the previous ten years. They claimed that the Popondetta Subdistrict had one suicide in 1955, one in 1959, and six in 1960, that the

Kokoda Subdistrict had two suicides in 1950, one each in 1953, 1954, 1955, 1957, 1959, and 1960, and three in 1961, and that the Tufi Subdistrict had one suicide in 1958. I formed the opinion that no specific pattern of variability could be derived from these figures, that not all suicides or attempted suicides were reported as such by the traditional peoples, that information on remote village deaths did not always reach the subdistrict office, and that coroners' inquiries were not always held. As far as I could see no dramatic change in the pattern of life of these rural people, the Orokaiva, had taken place in the previous decade. What is of interest is the predominance of females and the fact that derris-root poisoning was the preferred suicidal method. Of the twenty-one cases, no fewer than eighteen employed this method, and fifteen of these were females. Most were young girls whose parents would not allow them to marry the men of their choice. Marriage being an affair of state with a political basis, in most instances the assigned suitor was often an older man, and therefore less desirable. These cases were clearly of the hysterical gesture type, a common mode of attempted suicide employed by females in European countries. The difference is that the indigenous woman lacks the sophistication of her European counterpart in making the act fall just short of tragedy.

Derris root is known to the people as a potent fish poison and is employed extensively by them in the inland creeks and rivers. The root is macerated with the aid of a stone and exudes a milky fluid which in water brings the intoxicated fish to the surface. Its toxic properties account for its use as a suicidal instrument. Some women have been found dead with the root in their mouths. Derris root is widespread throughout New Guinea, where it is known popularly as New Guinea Dynamite. The active principle is rotenone, a crystalline neutral five-carbon-ring compound. Toxic doses produce vomiting, inco-ordination, clonic convulsions, muscular tremors, and death by depression of respiration.

Papua New Guinea has approximately one quarter of the world's languages. Each of the language groups is to some extent a group of differentiated culture, so that variation in the details of beliefs and attitudes, including those connected with suicide, is to be expected. There are, however, important points of similarity. Most groups are acephalous and lack centralized authority. All stress kinship and descent in the formation of local social structures. All practice agriculture to some extent; some are in addition pig-herders, hunters, and fishermen. A further point which all known groups have in common is the great extent to which supernatural beliefs influence their thinking. In a large number of socioeconomic activities, dependence on the assistance of supernatural agencies leads, particularly in some coastal peoples, to religious petitioning of these spiritual forces and to magical manipulation of the supernatural. Thus most illnesses or untoward events of significance in the lives of the people are thought to be due to the action of sorcerers, or of deities, demons, or ghosts. Most deaths, including suicide, are similarly explained, albeit retrospectively.

The magico-religious belief systems of the different peoples are similar in two main ways. The mind of the traditional person is untutored in western logic and scientific method. In his search for explanations of the world around him he has become animistic in his thinking, the physical and spiritual worlds being united into one comprehensive system. Therefore the movement from one phase to another is viewed less seriously than is the case with the white person. There is a grade of reality attributed to the spirit world that has little or no correlate in the mind of the sophisticated observer. The other world is supernatural only in a very limited sort of way. The deities, demons, and ghosts live near and around living people and may interfere in their affairs. Possession of the patient's body by alien spirits, loss of his own spirit, two spirits fighting for possession of the one body, and many other variants of human-spirit relationships are to be observed from time to time among indigenous patients, and not only among the nonliterate ones. These states are often associated with marked anxiety and panic, which lead at times to overt acts of suicide. It is also possible to set up a two-way human-spirit intercommunication whereby advice is sought and given. This may be effected by sleeping in the former house of the ancestral spirit in question.

The second way in which the Papua New Guinean belief systems are similar is that roughly the same types of spirit-beings are found throughout the country. They are deities, demons, and ghosts and are remarkably human and nonethereal in their behavior. Nevertheless the peoples' beliefs are profound, and as with other religious systems they are accorded the respect that is their due. Belief in immortality is widespread, although Highlands patients often show less enthusiasm in this way than coastal ones. A common characteristic of these beliefs, at least as far as we know about them in the clinical context, is their vagueness. There is a hard core of central belief which is subject to elaboration and embellishment by particular informants. Some interpretations may even be constructed during the course of interview. Some form of belief in reincarnation is not uncommon, and suicides have occurred to speed up the passage into the next world with the clearly defined objective of returning again at a later date.

Written codes and law-making bodies are not immediately obvious among the indigenous cultures. Those that do exist have been imposed from outside. Thurnwald (1929) has indicated that those New Guinea Societies with

which he was familiar acknowledged a set of rules governing human behavior and binding on the individual. Todd
(1935–36), in referring to the redress of wrongs among the
people of Möwehafen in New Britain, commented on the
strong kinship ties and lack of any central body of law. This
was a great weakness, making complete and satisfactory
rectifications unlikely, to the grave detriment of the individual. Williams (1941) considered that the behavior
transgressions of the people of Lake Kutubu of the Southern Highlands District of Papua were small wrongs rather
than big ones. They were in the nature of affronts, but
produced strong emotional responses, with humiliation
and loss of face, that could lead to suicide, not only in the
wrongdoer but also in the victim. Pospisil (1958) produced
the first detailed account of a New Guinea legal system in
his study of the Kapauku Papuans of West Irian. Many
features of their social life are similar to those of the High-
landers of the Trust Territory of New Guinea. He was
impressed by the developed systems of law operating in
the minds of the people. He concluded that a nucleus of
three people, the two disputants and an accepted ad-
judicator, was necessary for law to be said to exist in the
lives of members of the different cultural-linguistic
groups.

It was formerly a crime in the Western system to take
one's own life, hence the term *felo de se*. In earlier times
various religious discriminations and forfeiture of property were considered adequate deterrents. In Papua New
Guinea, the Queensland Criminal Code has been adopted.
The law relating to suicide under this code states that any
person who attempts to kill himself is guilty of a mis-
demeanor and is liable to imprisonment with hard labor
for one year. But the community turns a blind eye to this
provision. In the last ten years there have been only three
committals to the Supreme Court for attempted suicide.
Two were not proceeded with, and the accused in the third

instance was acquitted on account of insufficient evidence. During this period a fourth person, who tried to burn himself to death in a building, was charged with arson. The prosecutor did not proceed with the case. One of the two cases not proceeded with came from the remote area of Daru Island in the Western District of Papua. After selling his fishing catch one day the man went to a bar and had some alcohol. He returned to his dwelling and was using his young sister's lamp. She came and complained about this, saying that her husband was returning soon and would need it. According to local custom it is a very shameful thing for a younger sister to chastise an older brother. He was shamed, got a rope and put it over the branch of a mango tree and also around his neck. The village people cut him down before any great harm was done. In this instance there were no sanctions at the traditional level, nor any at the hands of the larger law of the state.

Papua New Guinea law in practice is thus seen as a blend of Australian law and indigenous law. Numerous ordinances and regulations have been consistently concerned with local customs, and the lower courts have been directed to apply such principles except where grossly contrary to the law of the state. The Native Customs (Recognition) Ordinance 1963 has greatly clarified the place of cultural factors. Under this ordinance indigenous custom is to be recognized, enforced by, and pleaded in all courts. In this context the court is not obliged to observe strict legal procedure, can include hearsay and expressions of opinion, and is to take indigenous custom into account in ascertaining the state of mind of an individual on a charge of suicide or on any criminal charge. The court is thus given the widest discretion and employs the method it considers best in the interests of justice.

The relatives of persons who attempt suicide show a wide spectrum of response to this form of behavior. There are those who say that we have to accept philosophically what has happened and that life must go on. They say it is the personality of the patient, and we must accept it as such. There are those who say that the attempt was a good thing, but in these cases one suspects an underlying hostility to the person concerned. Then there are those who say that it is a bad thing and that they are hostile towards him for making trouble with the government and for risking the loss of one of their members and so reducing the strength of the group. There are those who say that he is mad. And finally there are those who agree that suicide had to take place following shame for the transgression of some code and that the person concerned was a pretty poor type for having botched the job.

What of the attitudes of members of the group to the surviving relatives of successful suicides? In Marshall Lagoon they might blame the widow. Had she been hostile toward her husband? Did she have an affair with another man? Did she commit an act of sorcery by making "poison" (sorcery) against him so that he hanged himself? She remains under suspicion for a long time. There is a period of mourning of six months' duration, and if this is not fully observed, there will be those who will become very angry and suspicious concerning her involvement in his suicide. But they will be very careful if they feel that the survivor's sorcery is stronger than their own.

Despite the comforts of Christian religion, Australian cultural attitudes do not as yet permit facing and integrating the concept of death. The fact of death has not yet become part of the concept of living. Australian suicide remains surrounded by numerous taboos. These leave the person with feelings that the act is sinful, a sign of mental disorder, or the result of weakness of character. But in the magico-religious sytems of the indigenous people, in their efforts to orientate to their surroundings, their animism results in union of the spirit and physical worlds.

The group of affective psychoses in Papua New Guinea,

in their most obvious manifestations, take the form of recurrent manic reactions. The transcultural difficulties in the diagnosis of other forms of mental disorder are not met with here. These are the most culture-free of all the conditions examined; the diagnosis is comparatively easy and is often made by observation alone. True depressive responses are not readily seen and appear to be uncommon, although depressive equivalents may well be present in some of those disorders categorized as primarily psychoneurotic. The sociocultural dimension becomes important when we have to deal with shame reaction and shame suicide. The distinctive response of the nonliterate person to the real or expected social disapproval of the members of his own cultural-linguistic group has had applied to it the European label of shame. This is the distressing emotion associated with subjective awareness that one is likely to be ostracized, to be isolated by public criticism, and to receive punishment. It is a simple defensive reaction in which the subject may or may not look sad and may run away or commit suicide. It has certain similarities with the symptom of depression among white peoples, but the latter is a different type of compound affect formed by the fusion of such individual simple affects as grief, hurt, grievance, anxiety, and anger, often against a background of discrepancy between aspiration and achievement. The roots of shame are different. Shame as a symptom is short-lived, and when the person is communicative, it is revealed in the course of examination. It usually lacks the sustained, dismal, retarded character of the European affective psychosis. The presence or absence of shame in a potentially shame-producing situation is closely related to the social orbit of the individual, the cultural-linguistic group. The person concerned is unlikely to feel shame in relation to his identical transgressions outside his own group. For example, it's open season for the girl on the other side of the hill as far as rape is concerned, and one might boast about one's exploits in this connection. On this side, however, shame would be inevitable and would often lead to suicide.

In this country the *amok* runner, whom we shall describe in more detail later, is almost invariably a nonliterate bush person with suicide as one of his objectives. He experiences an identity crisis following an intolerable insult. As a poor man of lowly status, he concludes he has nothing to lose but his life, which is rated by others as of no importance. He kills to punish his offenders and to suffer the inevitable retribution. He thus reasserts himself in the eyes of the group and serves a death wish at the same time.

Not a few cargo cult leaders have been shown to suffer from some form of mental disorder. The following have been observed: epilepsy, hysteria, chronic syphilitic meningoencephalitis, *folie à deux*, grandiose paranoia, schizophrenia, affective psychosis, and thyrotoxic psychosis (Burton-Bradley 1970). Suicide may occur as part of any of these disease processes, or in their absence, in four main ways:

1. As a by-product of the disease process per se,
2. as a method to speed up the cargo process by magico-religious means,
3. as a method to emulate the Christian Passion, or
4. as a method to leave phase one of the cosmic process and enter phase two, for personal reasons to avoid an obligation, with the further view of returning again at a later date (phase three).

The distinguishing feature of the act of suicide among the mixed-race peoples is its rarity. Cross-cultural intermarriage is common. Its occurrence in the past is not surprising when we consider such factors as propinquity of the sexes, the radical disparity in the sex ratio of the dominant group favoring the male, and the propitious climate wherein the indigenous woman married into a higher social stratum. The towns were characterized by a changing and cosmopolitan population, custom was relaxed, and prescribed taboos governing mate selection were not rigorously enforced.

The innocent products of such unions did not always fare so well. They felt the full impact of society's attitude. Being midway between the alien and indigenous cultures, the members of both often treated them with indifference. The feasibility of establishing an enduring social orbit made up of a healthy pattern of interpersonal relationships was not very great. A variety of adaptive and maladaptive devices were employed in the alleviation of anxiety arising from such circumstances. Suicide was seldom one of them. Surrounded on all sides by denigration, the child of a cross-cultural marriage had understandably well developed ego defenses. Hypochondriasis was not uncommon. The white father, who was held responsible for the disliked caste position, was too prestigious a person towards whom to direct one's hostility, and the person's own organs, rather than the organism itself as a whole, received the brunt of the impact. Over the past five years new job and economic opportunities, improved quality of race relations, and the introduction of overseas capital have done much to alter the situation. It remains to be seen whether the suicide rate will change with the emerging new cultural values. The following two cases, which are the only ones known to me, concern individuals who have been exposed to long periods of alien European values.

A mixed-race adult male had been sent to Australia for higher education. He enjoyed this very much, feeling the manifestations of prejudice and discrimination to be barely discernible. This was particularly important, as he labored under a grave physical disability. He had good prospects, however. But on returning home he felt rejected and considered that his former caste status had been reimposed. He became aggressive and ended up in jail. On release, he shot himself.

Another mixed-race adult male, who was a professional man, after an apparently normal afternoon umpiring at cricket and enjoying some conviviality at the club had a disagreement with his wife and broke into the medical store of the outstation. He opened seven fifty-milligram ampoules of pethidine and was in the process of injecting their contents when arrested by the police for breaking and entering. He stated that he regarded the lethal dose of pethidine as two hundred and fifty milligrams.

The problems of mixed-race people have been described under the headings of "Marginal Personality" (Park 1928) and "Marginal Situation" (Dickie-Clark 1966). They refer to the cultural hybrid who shares the values of two distinct groups. Stonequist (1937) elaborated the characteristic features of their personality, laying great stress on self-hatred. In the light of these descriptions it is indeed surprising that suicide is so uncommon among the mixed-race people of this country. A personality structure based on ambivalence could well be important in this regard as limiting the final decision to commit the act.

The term *European* refers to the white residents. It is an odd usage in that very few come from the northern hemisphere, although many of their ancestors may have done so. They are mostly Australians with the additions of a few **New Zealanders, Englishmen,** so-called "New Australians," who are immigrants from abroad, and people from other Commonwealth countries. They come and go, live in a state of temporariness, and most are expatriation-oriented—that is, they recognize that the duration of their stay is limited, with the development of the country towards independence. Most work for the government, private enterprise, or the Christian missions or they are in the armed forces. Although they are in a new and strange environment and contribute greatly to the social and technological development of the country, as individuals and groups, they live in psychological enclaves, so powerful is the influence of their cultures of origin. Their suicide rate is the same as that of Australia, namely 13 per 100,000. The methods employed simulate those of Australia and differ only in the availability of means. Thus a woman may shoot herself with a rifle, an uncommon mode in the same social class in Australia. Although it has not been proven by any definitive study, Europeans are believed to drink alcohol to a greater extent than they would in their own country, and there is some evidence that alcohol is kept in houses ostensibly for social purposes by those who would not do so in their own homeland. Unstable personalities lacking the support of the home culture find comfort in excessive drinking in the tropics, and this is a feature to be noted in some cases of attempted suicide by lonely persons. Other cases include hysterical gestures with overdoses of barbiturates, shooting oneself out of fear of homosexual exposure, puerperal depression, schizophrenia, fear of retribution for gambling debts, guilt over cross-cultural liaisons, and sexual jealousies.

Taboo—neomelanesian *tambu*—is the widely used Oceanic term that refers to certain types of prohibition, the violation of which results in undesirable consequences. The indigenous people are rather vague when asked how the machinery works; what is important to them is that certain acts produce disagreeable results. These phenomena are culture-specific, and a knowledge of the various taboos against incest and postpartum sex and rules concerning kin avoidance is essential for their correct management. These taboos vary considerably among the various cultural groups. With the current intraterritorial migrations and the acceleration of social change taking place primarily as a result of contact with an alien culture, there is increased conflict arising from transgression of these codes, with consequent anxiety, maladaptation, and, in some cases, suicide. Malinowski (1959) gives a graphic account of a youth in the Trobriands who had broken the rules of exogamy, the partner in the transgression being his maternal cousin, the daughter of his mother's sister. The youth put on festive attire and ornamentation and jumped to his death from the top of a coconut tree sixty feet high.

The term *anomie* is used here to refer to a condition of personal disorganization in which two different sets of norms are in conflict and the person concerned fails in an attempt to conform to contradictory requirements, with consequent anxiety, low threshold for aggression, and, at times, suicide. The contract laborer on plantations who has come from afar, the detainee in the corrective institutions, the older bachelor seeking a niche, the refugee from the Indonesian province of Irian Jaya, and the retiring government employee returning to his culture of origin after a long absence are important examples of those most exposed to this particular hazard. It is usually associated with lack of ready access to kinsmen or with rejection by them. There are aggressive outbursts, short-lived psychotic or psychoneurotic episodes, and failed or successful suicides, in which the symptomatology lays stress on themes derived from the culture of origin. In its acute form this condition may be referred to as the Papua New Guinea transitory delusional state or transient situational disorder; more often the syndrome or symptom complex is of subacute character.

Alternative forms of self-destructive behavior that are partial or quasi suicides are not lacking where the person concerned has an unconscious need for self-punishment. Disease processes, such as pulmonary tuberculosis, in the indigene and the marginal personality structure of the mixed-race person are exploited as indirect expressions of self-destruction. An institutionalized form of homosexuality among certain Western District peoples who live in a poor physical environment can well be looked upon as a rationalization of similar underlying motives. Obesity in certain areas, violence, homicide, crime, and naïve forms of check forging that are foredoomed to failure can often be looked upon in the same way.

Many peoples, such as the Gimi and Fore of the Highlands and the Goilala of the Central District of Papua, perform self-amputation of parts of fingers while in mourning for dead relatives. This is widespread and is performed with great fortitude and a seemingly marked indifference to pain. A portion of the individual dies as the relative has done. It is effected by binding at the interphalangeal joints with a tight cord, so that the terminal portions become gangrenous and ultimately drop off. Another method is their quick dispatch with the aid of a tomahawk.

What can be done about the suicide situation as it exists at present, and what might be expected in the near future? Durkheim asserts that the total incidence of suicides for a culture is a social fact that is a function of the society in question. It stays at a remarkably constant level from year to year unless subject to unusual influences. Under these circumstances it would seem to be unrealistic to expect any great change in the pattern. Even if it were theoretically possible to make substantial inroads into the problem, our ability to do so would presuppose not only our knowing all the underlying social preconditions for suicide, but our being able in fact to remove them. But the problem is somewhat different in dealing with individual human beings, and much can be done in the case of those persons who are suicide prone, or who are detected as highly likely to commit suicide.

4 Amok

THE EXPLOSIVE reaction commonly referred to as *running amok* was originally thought of as being confined to the Muslims of Malaysia, Indonesia, and the Philippines. This view was reinforced by lack of reports emanating from China and other non-Muslim countries. Observations I have made among peoples of three grades of technological development, namely the Melanesians in Papua New Guinea, the Chinese in Singapore, and white Caucasians in Australia, would suggest that the identical syndrome transcends the narrow culture-bound definition. Furthermore, if we accept the four essential clinical criteria as postulated by the early writers (Gimlette 1901; Galloway 1923) of prodromal brooding, explosive homicidal outburst, continuing homicidal drive in absence of easily elicited motive, and a retrospective assertion of amnesia, then it is clear that the condition has a wide distribution indeed, both geographically and historically.

It is of interest to note that although the origin of the word *amok* is unknown, the Indian anthropologist Gaikwad (1970) has indicated that there is strong circumstantial evidence of its derivation from the Sanskrit. According to Fitzgerald (1923) the term *amok runner* was first used by the Anglo-Indians. The medical and anthropological literature records instances of the amok runner from many different countries, with greater prevalence in some geographical areas and with greater incidence during some historical periods. Accounts originate from the Indian subcontinent

(Masters 1920), the West Indies (Masters 1920), Siberia (Adams 1951), and Africa (Carothers 1953). When viewed historically, it is to be noted that Singaporean amok was reported more frequently in earlier decades than it was ten years ago. Today we seldom hear about it, there being only one very obvious case recently. Similar reports emanate from Indoncoia with rcopcct to that country. It io doubtful whether such a dramatic event, with its high visibility, could escape detection in these last two instances. Its great variability of concentration in time and place is indicative of its culture-relatedness and its sensitivity to cultural change. We note how the Moro of the Philippines often asks permission of his parents prior to running amok. Of considerable importance is the explanation given by Wulfften-Palthe (1933), for whom amok is a standardized form of emotional release, recognized as such by the community and, indeed, expected of the individual who is placed in an intolerably embarrassing or shameful position. He notes that there is no record of any case of amok occurring among many of the Malays living in Europe. He makes it quite clear that the Malaysian social structure, with its strong kinship ties, and the tensions arising from these obligations have a definite influence on the frequency, and he illustrates this point with reference to the old hospital in the Glodock district of Djakarta, with its typical nonliterate village-type atmosphere, where amok was quite common. He records that, when the patients were transferred to a new, modern, fully equipped hospital, where an entirely different atmosphere prevailed and kinship obligations were not so pressing, amok among the patients ceased.

As far as Papua New Guinea is concerned, amok has seldom been reported in the past. This is not surprising, in view of the history and terrain of the country and the paucity of pertinent records. In some popular writing in the early years of this century (Monckton 1921) reference is made to a supposed high incidence of mental illness in the d'Entrecasteaux group of islands in Eastern Papua. The author describes three cases of members of his party or villagers running amok while he was on patrol. He also expressed the opinion that amok was not uncommon in Northern Papua, where it seemed to be accepted by the rest of the village as well as by the patient himself as a recognized form of emotional response. According to a cultural anthropologist (Fortune 1932), amok was a well-known occurrence on the island of Dobu in Eastern Papua, where he observed actual instances three times within six months. In his view, amok was closely related to sorcery. This is not surprising and is in line with his assessment of the culture in that area as having strong paranoid components.

I have had the opportunity of studying the cases described below. Apart from these, there have been numerous other instances which could be described either as abortive cases or as partial components of the condition in which some intervening situation prevented their full expression. The recorded instances represent only a small fraction of the totality of violence, including multiple violent acts, that have been presented for medical assessment over the past decade. None of the subjects exhibited evidence of eplilepsy, overt schizophrenia, or any other form of mental disorder. All were in good physical health, although a recent history of brief exposure in the jungle was not uncommon. All the Papua New Guinea cases were young adult males, single or married, laborers, village gardeners, or artisans. None had any schooling; all could be considered as only partially acculturated. A summary of the cases in the form of a clinical amalgam gives the following type of picture. A healthy young adult is quieter than usual or "goes bush," as it is termed, for a few days. There is a history of insult, defined as such by the individual himself. He may regain his normal composure, or the condition may continue and remain unchanged as an abortive attack, or it may become worse. In the last instance, suddenly without warning, he jumps up, seizes an axe or some spears, rushes around attacking all and sundry and even destroying inanimate objects, such as yam houses or hospital property. Within a short period a number of persons will be dead or wounded. He shouts that he is going to kill and everyone in the neighborhood seeks safety in flight. All are fully aware that the man is suffering from a special form of *longlong* or *kavakava* and that he will not be satiated or stop of his own accord. They recognize that this and similar types of reaction are available methods of tension reduction, used from time to time as acts arising from despair. The man continues in this fashion until overpowered, by which time he has become exhausted. He may also be killed or wounded. The attack may be aborted at any time by anyone who is brave enough to attempt it. On his recovery, the man asserts that he has no memory of the event.

I have discussed the circumstances with those amok runners who survived, with their relatives, and with other Papua New Guineans, and I have appeared in court as an expert witness to assist with the defense. On the basis of the data derived from these sources, I am of the opinion that the individual's mode of thinking is somewhat as follows and I express it here for convenience in transcultural paraphrase:

> I am not an important or "big" man. Although poor, I have always had my sense of personal dignity and social identity. But I have had little else. Now even this has been taken from me and my life reduced to nothing by an intolerable insult. Therefore, I have nothing to lose except my life, which is rated as nothing, so I trade my life for yours as your life is favored. The exchange is in my favor, so I shall not only kill you, but I will kill many of you, and at the same time I will rehabilitate myself in the eyes of the

group of which I am a member even though I might be killed in the process.

The evidence suggests that the killings are envisaged as a means of deliverance from an unbearable situation. No doubt much sullen meditation precedes the nihilistic feeling of desperation—kill or be killed. At some point, however, there is complete loss of control, when strong emotion becomes unchecked by deliberation and reflection.

What can be said concerning the etiology of this condition? At the time of the earlier descriptions epilepsy was a strong contender. The epistemic paradigms of the day were greatly under the influence of the English neurologist Hughlings Jackson, whose eminence was such that even culturally oriented Kraepelin, who had traveled widely in the Far East, tended to view the syndrome as the manifestation of an epileptic dream state. Since that time occasional observers have noted in passing the wounded self-esteem of individuals and the social expectancies of the kinsfolk. Betel intoxication, malaria, pneumonia, syphilitic meningoencephalitis, hypoglycemia, head injury, heat exhaustion, and schizophrenia have all been implicated by various authors. The impact of Hughlings Jackson and the organic emphasis peculiar to the discipline of tropical medicine have monopolized the scene until the mid-twentieth century. A premature disclosure of the plot to be presented will, I hope, add clarity to the understanding. Accordingly, *the cases I report here and elsewhere, including those I consider abortive, lead me to postulate a sociopsychodynamic explanation which points to the overriding significance of the patient-defined unrelieved insult in a context of group expectancies.* I shall now illustrate this theme by reference to examples drawn from each of the three grades of technological development to which I have referred. The principals in the following examples are Melanesians of Papua New Guinea.

A young adult male indigene from Mapamoiwa, Fergusson Island, on admission to hospital said that he had killed an old man and a young *meri* (woman) and speared three others. He said that he must have done this because people said that this was what he had done, and therefore it must be so; but that he himself had no clear recollection of the detail. He said that he did not have anything against any of these people and that they had done him no harm. He said that he had been in the bush without food for two days prior to the offense. On further examination of the patient it was clear that his amnesia was not absolute, as he had originally said, and he indicated that at the time of the offense he was aware that his actions might lead to death and that they were wrong both in the eyes of his people and in those of the administration. An eyewitness said that he was sitting in front of his house with some of his relatives at about seven o'clock on the night of the episode, when he saw the patient standing about twenty-five feet away from the group. It was dusk, and there was light from the cooking fire. The patient had a spear, which he raised and threw at them, and it hit one of them in the side. The victim was carried inside, and while this was being done, another spear hit another member of the group, who withdrew the spear from her own body. Everyone ran away, and in the process some had to defend themselves. The patient said: "Where are you all? I am coming after you." The eyewitness then hid until daybreak, when he found two bodies, one inside and one under the house. Then, with five other villagers, he searched for the patient, who was found in the bush, having been wounded in the chest and on the head. He had five spears stuck in the ground standing up beside him. He was overpowered. In addition to attacking and killing people while running around, he had damaged and destroyed yams in the yam house. After his admission to hospital, no evidence of any other form of mental disorder was detected. This case illustrates the full syndrome and emphasizes the supposed lack of direction of the act.

A healthy young adult male, who originally came from the hinterlands of Abau, Central District, was working with a building gang on Fergusson Island. He was a foreigner to his workmates, one of whom called him an "Abau bush pig"—a grave insult. One night at about six-thirty, the others were in their dormitory reading or lying down, when the patient came in with a twelve-inch bush knife and suddenly attacked them, going from bed to bed hacking at them with the knife, mostly in the vicinity of the head and neck. Six died then or later, some with terrible wounds, their heads being almost chopped off. Finally, another man in the vicinity heard the noise and came in with a rifle and one cartridge. The amok runner attempted to attack him, was fired at, and still did not cease attacking. He was then put out of action by the butt of the rifle and died. This case was aborted by the killing of the amok runner. It also illustrates the gravity of the insult, which he considered to be intolerable.

A healthy, athletic young adult Orokaivan, a carpenter, had been working in a district town. He became homesick and decided to return. He had almost reached his destination, after a long walk of some fifty miles over a number of days, when he entered a village where he was known. Suddenly he sprang up and attacked the man who had offered him a meal, shouting that he was going to kill him. He picked up an axe, and the man ran away. A village dog bit him, and he then chased the dog and some children, who were in their canoes on the river. He grabbed an empty canoe and endeavored to chase and capture them, without success. He returned to the shore, and with an axe and spears chased anyone he could find, eventually spearing a woman in the back and a man in the thorax with a four-pronged fishing spear. According to the village people, there had been no provocation, only friendliness. He

was then hit with a stone, overpowered and handed over
to the police. He refused to eat and drink, was admitted to
hospital where he was given electroconvulsive treatment
and tube-fed, after which he started eating and·was shortly
ready for discharge from hospital. During the following
twelve months he was examined frequently, and no form
of mental disorder was detected. He claimed to have only a
hazy memory of the acute phase. This case illustrates prodromal isolation in the bush, explosive and continued violence, and a claimed amnesia. The asymptomatic pre-amok
and post-amok history points to the absence of any mental
disorder other than the amok syndrome. His refusal to eat
was related to fear of retribution on a payback basis.

An adult male indigene of the eastern Highlands in the
Chuave Subdistrict was admitted to hospital after an outburst of violence, in which he attempted to attack the men,
women, and children in his immediate vicinity with an axe
and some spears and to destroy property without apparent
cause. His kinsfolk said that he had been unusually quiet
for several days before the attack. No one was killed, but
several persons were gravely injured. The amok runner
was overpowered by his kinsmen and tied up prior to
being brought to hospital. On examination, the patient
denied all recollection of the occasion and was then completely free of any signs of psychiatric illness. The patient
was transferred to the rehabilitation annex of the hospital.
There was no further disturbance until one month later,
when he became quiet and appeared to be brooding; he
suddenly took hold of a fishing spear which was lying in
the vicinity and attacked both staff and patients until he
was overpowered. Again the patient denied recollection of
the event. Staff members insisted that, had they not locked
themselves in a building, at one stage someone would
have been killed. No evidence of any other form of mental
disorder was detected, and his physical health was excellent. He claimed that he was skilled as a warrior and had
killed many men in intergroup warfare. This case illus-

trates the phenomenon of the war amok of the group reappearing in the behavior of an individual on two occasions in another context.

An adult male indigene from Tari Subdistrict in the southern Highlands was admitted to hospital with a history of having suddenly started attacking and wounding other people in his immediate vicinity with a knife and axe for no apparent reason. The attack was aborted by injuries inflicted on the amok runner by a man who protected himself with the aid of a bush knife. The patient subsequently denied all recollection of the occasion, other than saying that a kinsman had shown him a knife and that he remembered someone's accusing him of having had sexual intercourse with his mother. A grave insult preceded this running amok, which was aborted in the early phases.

A young adult male Goilala indigene was employed as a painter in a newly constructed swimming pool in Port Moresby, when he suddenly dropped his paint brush and started throwing house bricks at persons in the vicinity, continuing to do so until he was overpowered by the other workers. He claimed to have no recollection of the outburst, and his fellow workers said that there had been no provocation. It is significant, however, that in their eyes he was a foreigner. Within half an hour there was no evidence of any other abnormality. The stereotype of the Goilala as a dangerous foreigner is a widespread belief among other people in Papua. In this instance, there may have been expectations of the employment of the amok tension-reducing device which was aborted by overpowering the amok runner.

A young adult male Chimbu from the eastern Highlands was brought to hospital by the police, with a history of suddenly attacking his fellow workers, chasing them with an axe in one hand and a knife in the other, and saying that he was going to kill them. He was overpowered, however. It was stated that he had brooded for several days after being insulted by another worker, who said he was a "rubbish man" (a recognized form of abuse in this area, meaning somebody who is "good for nothing"), and had thrown water in his face. He claimed amnesia and was otherwise asymptomatic. This case exemplifies brooding after an insult, the subject being overpowered in the early stages.

I shall now refer to two Chinese amok runners whom I examined in Singapore during the nineteen-fifties Both instances were identical on all cardinal points with classical Malay amok. Both individuals were ethnically and culturally Chinese.

A forty-five-year-old male Henguha born in China came to Singapore when he was fourteen years old. He was unable to read or write. Despite this drawback, he was promoted to the position of workshop foreman. He stated that he had always been honest and that his boss had trusted him. Just prior to the incident he was suspended on the accusation that he had stolen some money. This he vigorously denied. A discussion ensued between two officials of the company. One wanted to dispense with his services; the other was doubtful. He felt insulted because of this. A few days later he went to the office to make a telephone call and a clerk made a gesture of spitting, saying that he was not a man. He brooded over this, saying, "Why should they insult me?" He went away and came back later with an axe and is alleged to have attacked all within reach, hitting them on the face, neck, and thorax. Three were killed in the process and two others seriously injured. He then set fire to the building and ran away. He was arrested, and on examination he showed no evidence of any form of mental or physical disorder then or later, other than that of the amok syndrome as described above. He first claimed amnesia for the event, saying that he was a trishaw driver and not a foreman, and that he did not know where the event took place, but this denial was followed by a statement indicating his occupation and confessing that he had picked up the axe and fought his way through the people.

A fifty-seven-year-old Chinese boatbuilder came to Singapore from Shanghai as a young man. On the afternoon of the incident he returned home after distributing some cards of invitation to his eldest son's forthcoming wedding. He appeared to be upset. His eldest son, thinking that his father was tired and "heated up inside," offered to buy him a "cooling drink." He refused and left. He did not return to sleep that night, and although his eldest son went to look for him at his favorite haunts, he did not find him. The next day he returned and knocked incessantly at the door of his neighbor's house, but there was no answer. A carpenter working nearby asked him what he wanted. Without answering a word, he attacked the carpenter with a piece of wood. He then picked up a chisel and attacked an old man standing nearby, stabbing him in the abdomen. This old man later succumbed to the injury. He continued in this way, attacking the old man's wife and granddaughter. He went to a sawmill and stabbed two men, then went into another house, where he attacked two women and a man. From here he rushed to a carpentry shop, stabbing another woman, and disappeared. Later he tried to drown himself in a river but was seen by the police and arrested. He still retained both the chisel and the piece of wood in his hands. In all, thirteen persons had been attacked. All were from Shanghai. Two men died and six others were seriously wounded. The rest had lesser injuries. The man claimed amnesia during the earlier stages following arrest. Later, in explanation, he stated that he was insulted on two occasions while distributing the wedding cards. He stated that he was driven away with contempt. This he saw as a wrong thing to do to an old man. He then stated that his mind was perfectly clear at the time of the killings and that if had his time over he would do exactly the same again.

Caucasians are not immune to the amok response. The case of Leo Held that occurred in Pennsylvania, in October

1967 (*Time*, November 3, p. 15; *Newsweek*, November 6, p. 36), also provided the model for the last case recounted below. Similar episodes clinically consistent with the full syndrome occur every five years or so in Australia and its dependencies. I report two cases here because of their intrinsic interest and for the possible value in prediction of the clues they supply. In the first one I was in the vicinity at the time of the outburst; in the second I was intimately concerned with the management.

A thirty-nine-year-old employed Caucasian mine worker had emigrated to Australia from Europe in 1939. The episode occurred in 1955. He had been to see four doctors seeking a compensation certificate for an alleged back injury. When the certificate was not forthcoming, he shot two of them dead and seriously wounded a third. The fourth had a lucky escape. He dodged the man and ran away. Then the amok runner blew himself up with a homemade bomb in the surgery of the fourth doctor, who had been marked out as the final victim. The whole episode was enacted within ten minutes, during which the man ran from one building to another in order to achieve his objective. He left a letter for the police in which he stated that he had no grudge against anyone else. The letter also showed that he had modeled his plans on the shooting of a doctor in Canada which had taken place a month previously. He had read about it in the newspaper. The victim of the Canadian shooting was an orthopedic specialist and the killer was one of his patients. This man had walked into the doctor's surgery while the doctor was treating patients, had pulled a rifle from his coat, and had fired at the doctor, killing him instantly.

When such an event as this occurs, we should be especially alert for the possibility of other outbursts. Furthermore, no compensation seeker should ever be considered a "humbug," which was the term alleged to have been used by one of the doctors.

A thirty-five-year-old Caucasian public servant had emigrated to Australia from Europe as a young man. He claimed to have had no significant promotion for a period of ten years. I came into the picture in 1967 when he wrote me a letter outlining a claim of differential treatment. He stated that he had been continually overlooked, that colleagues with the same or lesser qualifications had been promoted, and that he had been railroaded into a dead-end position. This he felt was beyond endurance. He stated his empathy with, and total acceptance of, the solution adopted by a laboratory technician from Pennsylvania who had recently run amok, killing six persons and wounding six others. This had been reported in great detail in the weekly newspaper. Most of the victims either were in authority over him or had been promoted while he had not. As he lay dying following a gun battle with the police, his last words were: "I had one more to go." I asked the public servant to come and see me, and during the course of the interview I detected oversensitivity coupled with anxiety and anger. I formed the opinion that he had a diminished capacity to select and control alternative forms of behavior. There was, I felt, a serious risk that he would act out the Pennsylvania model. I told him I would look into the situation and report back to him. I then conferred with his superiors, and it transpired that his promotion was in fact being processed, but at a very slow bureaucratic rate. This was speeded up, and the would-be amok runner informed, with dramatic effect in eliminating his brooding. When examined almost two years later, he was free of all symptoms.

I shall now comment on the forensic aspects. It is clear that each individual case suspected to be one of amok or quasi amok should be assessed on its merits. Although the classical syndrome is fairly clear-cut, some cases are of dubious nature, and there will be the added problem of dealing with supposed contributing factors. The apparent lack of motive and the asserted amnesia will need special attention. For the purpose of forming an opinion, the questions which must be answered are as follows: Does the person suffer from a state of mental disease or natural mental infirmity? Nosological niceties are not required, since the court will accept the fact of disease when, from whatever cause, the functions of the understanding are thrown into derangement or disorder. Such disease may be mental or physical and either temporary or permanent. In terms of this definition, classical amoks can be regarded as suffering from mental disease. Nonclassical amoks may not necessarily be so regarded.

If the answer to the first question is in the affirmative, can it be regarded as more probable than not that, as a result of mental disease or natural mental infirmity, the supposed amok runner did not know what he was doing or that it was wrong? Or even if he knew these things, was he unable to control his actions? Or was he under the influence of a delusion as to what he was doing, so that had the delusion been true, his act would not have been wrongful? In the examination of such a person, the first thing the doctor will do will be to determine whether in fact mental disorder or any physical disease process was present at the time of the act in question. He will carry out a full psychiatric and physical examination, including a full blood count and X-ray examination of the lung fields. In particular, he will have blood films examined for malaria parasites before administering suppressants. He will endeavor to determine whether there was knowledge at the time in question of the nature of the act—that is to say, that the activities would result in death. He will determine whether or not there had been knowledge (cognizance) of the harmfulness and wrongfulness of the act, both in the eyes of the people of the defendant's own culture and also in the eyes of the administration. The question will arise whether there was an element of premeditation. Psychiatric examination may be able to reveal whether the defendant was able to form an intent. Usually there have been several days of brooding when this has been possible, but these days have often been spent in the bush without food or shelter. In short, the defendant may have suffered from exposure and hunger, with possible impairment of ability to form conscious intent. Confronted with the claim of amnesia for the period of the killings, the examiner will remember that there are a number of other possibilities—namely, malingering, hysterical reaction, other forms of psychosis, epilepsy, drug intoxication and head injury. When the prospect of a feigned amnesia is under consideration, an exact note should be made of what the defendant says about the events of the killing. He may know more than he says and may reveal this fact unintentionally, or he may say "everything went red," or "everything went black," or "I remember nothing; I see that I am jail and if you say I killed these people, then it must be so." The diagnosis of malingering will be made only if the other possibilities are excluded and if there is, in addition, positive evidence of malingering apart from such an exclusion. Malingering may be defined as a deliberate feigning of illness in order to avoid an obligation or to gain a privilege. The examiner should be sensitive to, and make allowances for, his own subjective responses and prejudices derived from the current social values of the group from which the examiner comes in assessing a supposed instance of malingering. A feigned amnesia has a patchy and self-serving quality not present in genuine amnesia. To implicate hysterical reactions, it is necessary to demonstrate the previous occurrence of episodes of this kind or the presence of a known hysterical personality, as well as showing that the outburst is consistent with a coexistent trance or fugue.

The formal psychiatric examination may have established the presence of a previous psychosis and, if such is the case, it would be necessary to show, on the presumption of its continuity, that it was operative at the time in question. Epilepsy has often been alleged to be associated with an attack of amok, and the examiner needs objective evidence of the presence of ictal phenomena. In practice, this usually means the direct observation of a petit mal or grand mal seizure by a trained person on this or some previous occasion. The observations of untrained persons in respect to epilepsy in the jungle context are virtually useless. The presence of large burn scars on a highlands subject is almost diagnostic. Betel-nut chewing is widespread, and the defendant may have been chewing at the time. Its pharmacological action is that of producing euphoria; there is clarity of consciousness, with an increased capacity for work, so that its value as a defense at law is unlikely to be very great. Very rarely betel-nut chewing is associated with a psychosis, in which case it would be necessary to demonstrate, for example, the presence of hallucinations or delusions. Head injury needs special attention, as the amok often becomes injured during the course of the attack.

The apportionment of responsibility in the case of the individual supposed to be an amok runner is always difficult. The examiner should look at the totality of the situation. The more the symptomatology and total picture correspond to the classical description, the less likely is the individual to be legally responsible for his actions. If the cardinal symptoms—namely, prodromal brooding, outburst with homicidal intent, persistence in this fashion without apparent reason and claimed amnesia—are present, and the amok is committed without any possible motive at the time of the offense, without profit to the subject or others, without premeditation immediately prior to the explosion (although it may have existed earlier and is unlike any other form of criminality or psychosis), then it is unlikely that the amok could reasonably be considered criminally responsible for any death, injury, or destruction of property that may ensue.

The cases cited are characterized by the occurrence of a patient-defined unrelieved insult preceding the preliminary brooding and therefore cannot be considered as entirely without motivation, as claimed in the conventional descriptions. Nor is the amnesia absolute, as has also been claimed. In some accounts the action is said to be undirected. An explosive reaction may well involve every animate or inanimate thing in its path. Nevertheless, the claim of undirectedness should not be taken too literally, since the subject by his own actions places himself in a situation where an appropriate series of objects is present, and what he actually does clearly symbolizes his case against the group. The prior collection of weapons and the common social character of the members of the group attacked are facts hardly consistent with the claims. It is not enough to be satisfied when someone says he cannot remember, nor is a motive necessarily absent when it cannot be demonstrated. These matters must be determined by fact and not by inference. Detailed and prolonged clinical examination of amok survivors in hospital over a period of time is an essential prerequisite to a proper understanding. The following questions will have to be answered: When did the supposed amnesia commence? When did it end? Was it present all the time? Did it commence prior to the event and continue unabated? Was the alleged memory loss related only to the crime as such, or to all attendant circumstances? How many weapons did the subject say he collected beforehand, and what did he say he did with them later? Did the account given vary with the passage of time, and if so, in what way?

There are now something of the order of some three hundred and fifty papers in the literature on amok and related states (Smith 1957), which is an interesting fact in itself. Many of these tend to repeat what has been said before, often with a romantic flavor. Others are of more serious nature, and we are left roughly with two trends of thought, one which stresses the organic side and the other which lays greater emphasis on the psychogenic and socio-cultural side. In addition to this, psychiatrists of the areas referred to are heirs to the classification systems of both Continental Europe and England. Although these classifications do not refer directly to amok as such, it is clear that amok would be regarded as a psychogenic psychosis, a category appearing in the Continental European system but one which does not appear in the English system. My sociopsychodynamic position follows the psychogenic psychosis interpretation except that my clinical and forensic experience leads me to doubt the existence of any substantial amnesia. Although very brief amnesic phenomena may or may not be present, an efficient barrister can (and often does) readily produce irrefutable evidence exploding the postulate of a substantial amnesia. I am quite happy to concede that observers in other parts of the world may report on the presence in some instances of associated organic states during the occurrence of an amok response and that these states could well lower the threshold of reaction as aggravating factors. But such observers have yet to establish a clear nexus between any organic state and amok at the level of primary (rather than secondary) etiological importance. This is clear from the existence of those amok responses in which the amok runner has survived and whose examination immediately afterwards has revealed no organic pathology and no other psychiatric disorder.

Whatever the importance of any associated organic state, which if present must be diagnosed and treated in any case, it is clear that its relationship to the totality of the situation is largely that of a red herring. The amok runner lives in a restricted social orbit. His vision of the world at large is of a limited sort. He has his special needs, his special definition of the situation, and his special relationship to the group or subgroup of which he is a part. He assesses the position as one in which he has less to lose than others, and, as we have already indicated, the act symbolizes his case against the group.

A recognition of these facts by the practicing clinician and others is of importance in the field of prevention. So also is a proper understanding of the subject's culture as it colors the clinical picture. The Tamil laborer in Singapore who brings his brooding kinsman to the doctor requesting that he be locked up to avoid an amok outburst, the Moro of the Philippines who asks permission of his parents prior to running amok, and the Caucasian denied a deserved promotion in a context he defines as one of differential treatment are clearly worthy of close attention. One would hope, too, that the mass media will find ways and means of ensuring a more subdued reporting of these outbursts than has been the custom in the more recent past. Freely supplied models of behavior for the potential amok runner are clearly undesirable.

What can be said concerning the status of amok as a culture-bound reactive syndrome? It is clear that this condition is not bound to any specific culture in any absolute sense. The most we can say on the basis of existing information is that it appears to be much more common in some cultures than in others, and possibly absent from still others. And it appears to vary considerably in incidence within specific cultures at different points of historical time. Group expectancies foster its appearance where there is an amok tradition. The classification of amok as a unique type of mental disorder peculiar to a given culture would thus seem to be unwarranted. What is of significance to the psychiatrist is that it yields readily to analysis in terms of the categories of psychopathology.

5 Mixed-Race Marginality

THE TERMS *mixed-race* and *mixed-blood* are pejorative, and all reasonable persons look forward to the time when they will disappear altogether. In the meantime they are widely used by the Papua New Guinea mixed-race community, who seem on the whole to prefer the first self-assigned designation to the second. Such dual identity creates serious problems and will continue to do so until finally submerged into the burgeoning new nationalism.

For my purpose here, I refer to the person who thinks of himself as mixed-race and is considered as such by others. Such a definition implies an extraterritorial component in the ancestry. This is important when considering the person who is wholly descended from the indigenous inhabitants of the country, excluding those of wholly European or Asian descent, but whose parents have origin in different parts of Papua New Guinea. Such a person has been variously and quaintly referred to as an intertribal offspring, as being of an interbred tribe, or as *hap cas*. In former times such a person might assert that his biological status justified classification as mixed-race for purpose of exploiting the then existing discriminatory liquor rights, the mixed-race salary, which was higher, and the prestige that went with these acquisitions. This person had a marginal status of a different kind from that to be described.

Genes from overseas have probably been introduced since the earliest times. Although little is known of the situation that existed prior to the middle of the nineteenth century, the list of explorers reported to have touched the region is formidable. Since the discovery attributed to the Portuguese in 1511, they include the following (according to Legge 1955): De Retes (1546), Torres (1606), Tasman (1643), Dampier (1700), Carteret (1767), Bougainville (1768), Cook (1770), d'Entrecasteaux (1793), d'Urville (1827 and 1840), Blackwood (1842), Yule (1845), Owen Stanley (1846), Miklouho-Maclay (1871), and Moresby (1873). Mixed-bloods relate a story told by their elders concerning the people of Hood Point Peninsula, sixty miles east of Port Moresby. Before the Europeans came a Chinese boat was wrecked, and two of the Chinese crew were allowed to marry two widows. The rest were eaten. Certainly, representatives of these people with distinct Mongoloid features are to be seen today carrying in the fish at Koke Market, Port Moresby. Among the mixed-bloods themselves, the claimed ancestry is impressive. Countries of origin are stated by them to include Australia, Ceylon, China, Eire, Fiji, France, Germany, Greece, Guam, India, Indonesia, Italy, Malaya, the Middle East Countries, New Zealand, the Philippines, Portugal, the United Kingdom, Russia, the South Sea Islands, and Timor.

From the early part of the nineteenth century the region attracted escaped convicts, shipwrecked sailors, whalers, and traders. But it was not until the advent of white people and missionary influence that the seeds were sown for the establishment of the group of mixed-race people as herein defined, and we learn that a despatch from Deputy Commissioner Romilly to Sir Peter Scratchley in 1885 indicated that the former had deported two Europeans, whose seduction of indigenous females had caused him some concern (Legge 1955). According to Lett, Sir Hubert Murray, the Administrator, had a long acquaintance with a certain Louis Pothier, an escapee from the French convict settlement of Devil's Island (Lett 1949). He was impressed by Pothier's wishing to marry an unprepossessing Kiwai woman, who seemed to be "as mad as a March Hare." Pothier's daughter subsequently went to school in Australia; when ultimately she returned, she was faced with the difficulties associated with the mixed-blood status in the local society. By the end of 1890, provision had been made for a force of native constabulary, and two Fijians and twelve Solomon Islanders had arrived in Port Moresby. This was the result of the efforts of Sir William Macgregor, who also settled various members of his boat crew on blocks of land. The missions brought in Samoans and Filipinos. Also small ships from Australia with foreign crews came along, and the crew members drifted up to the goldfields and remained there. This sort of settlement began about 1884, dwindling out in the 1920s; thus, it went on for about thirty-six years. Propinquity and disparity in the sex ratio encouraged these men to establish liaisons with the indigenous women. Later the European trader gradually drifted in and gave rise to the "European mixed-blood" stock. It was during Sir Hubert Murray's administration that the notion of white superiority gathered strength, that the Europeans were split into fraternizers and nonfraternizers, and that the mixed-blood found himself, now clearly for the first time, to be rejected by the white group. His rejection by the indigenous group was to develop later in association with the education of the latter. In this situation mothers did not promote their children's education, preferring to hide and protect them. Poor schooling and their associated physiognomy resulted in their being given jobs by the planters and traders as so-called apprentices. Their good spoken English at this stage gave them a slight advantage over the indigenes. During the Pacific war, on 7 August 1942, the ship *Mamutu*, which was carrying a boatload of mixed-bloods, was sunk by enemy action. One survivor lives in Port Moresby.

Older mixed-bloods assert that there are four distinct

historical eras of mixed-blood drinking, a cardinal feature of their social life. Before 1948 there was total prohibition, during which there was illegal drinking. This was followed by the permit time (1948–1956), when selected mixed-blood persons were given permits by the Government Secretary following applications to, and reports from, the police regarding their character. These two eras were marked by a similar pattern of drinking and, compared with the third, described below, were noted for better community activity and more interest in sport. Dances were run better and were free of strife, drinking by young people under twenty-one years of age was frowned upon, and orderly picnics were popular. The third stage from 1956 onwards, was one of complete freedom, in which there was an initial upsurge of drinking which settled down to an over-all increase over that of previous periods. The final period was distinguished by the granting of liquor rights to indigenous people, thus removing for all time this status-conferring attribute from the mixed-blood.

Slow transformation has been going on all the time, but ten years after the war the position of the mixed-blood underwent visible change, since which time the transformation has been quite rapid. In 1954 six mixed-bloods were chosen to meet the Queen of England in Australia. The Mixed-Race Association was formed in 1955, the Island Social Club for women in 1959, and the Youth Club in 1960. A claim of $10,000 for breach of promise was made in 1961 by a twenty-five-year-old mixed-blood woman against a European man. During the same year the first marriage between a female European and a male indigene took place.

The mixed-race people are a marginal group in unstable equilibrium between the alien and indigenous cultures. They are a people without a culture, except in nascent form. The Europeans tend to disown them as half-castes and treat them with indifference and sometimes with disdain. With few exceptions they were not admitted to membership in European clubs until recent times. From the Papuan point of view there is no place in their cultural system for a person of mixed race. The Papuans resent the mixed-race man's superior attitude when he visits the village of his mother and his higher wages and former drinking privileges. They also have contempt for anybody who does not own property in land and who is not rooted in his own land and people. Originally the mixed-race people were a group of picturesque interest, but with the coming of white women and the creation of a more stable white society, they were soon confronted with rejection by a privileged class attempting to maintain its solidarity. In due course, also, they were to be excluded from indigenous benefits as the result of official preoccupation with the indigenous majority.

Upper-class mixed-race people are aware of the recent improvements in race relations. They say that formerly in shops, paper cups or pink-bottomed drinking glasses were reserved for Papuan and mixed-race people, although it might be different if the latter were personally known. Europeans were served with plain glasses reserved for them. Such discriminatory treatment no longer exists. Some fifteen years ago segregation was the main mechanism of racial discrimination, and in most instances it was buttressed by the law. Apart from social discrimination in schools, clubs, hotels, and cinemas, there was legal discrimination in respect to alien registration, wages, and national status. Improvement in these connections is obvious, and some say that progress is at times so fast as to create confusion. Physical segregation, however, persists. Separate mixed-race communities exist in fairly well defined areas of Gabutu, Hohola, Koke, Badili, Vabukori, Sixmile, and Bomana. Mixed-race people tend to seek acceptance among their own rather than live in isolated family groups among the European population, except in the more recent case of Boroko.

The status accorded to living in Australia is high. Upper-class mixed-race people explain it thus. There is no discrimination in Australia, they say, unlike Port Moresby, although it is not as bad there as before. Acts of discrimination, however mild, seem to have more significance for women than men; women react more, and may become furious.

Upper-class mixed-race people are often entertained by Europeans at official functions but rarely in their own homes. They also say that this discrimination is learnt. They have notice Europeans who, when they first came to the country to work, were friendly toward those of mixed race, but shortly they altered their approach to a polite nod only. They believe that this is due to the newcomers' being sensitized to such behavior patterns by the older European residents. On the other hand, Europeans who have felt a responsibility to correct this situation have reported rebuffs and vacillating responses to their overtures.

Papuans resent the two major privileges of the mixed-race community which they did not formerly enjoy. These are drinking rights (accorded to Papuans and New Guineans in the latter part of 1962) and mixed-race rates of pay (now disappearing with the general development of skills). Mixed-race people retort that Papuans have advantages in respect to rent, water, electricity, sanitation, fuel for cooking, financial aid for education or to start a business or build a house, and land.

Most cinemas now admit persons of all races. Several years ago, however, active discrimination against mixed-race people was the rule, they claim. They were sometimes refused admission. Apologies were given if subsequent complaints were made. Late in 1962 the final row of seats on one theatre was always kept empty, and on occasion mixed-race and Papuan people were shepherded to these seats. One mixed-race cinema fan told me that he did not enter the theatre until the lights went out.

Upper- and middle-class mixed-race people are highly sensitive to manifestations of prejudice and discrimination, however mild. They have a third ear in this connection, a feature closely allied to their genuine consideration for the feelings of others. For many of the lower class, discrimination does not constitute an important feature in their lives, and those who live like Papuans only respond as mixed-race persons when threatened with classification as natives. In this situation only are they really conscious of differential treatment.

In the view of older mixed-race people, there was greater mixing and good will between European and mixed-race people before the Second World War than there was later. There were fewer people, and wages for all were low. After the war, in the decade 1945–1955, relationships had reached their nadir, and informants refer to the period with distaste.

The mixed-race person has what some refer to as a natural caution. He does not wish to embarrass Europeans if he can avoid it. He will go out of his way (and act to his own disadvantage) to avoid such situations, because, he says, he does not like being embarrassed himself. On the other hand, some Papuans and New Guineans will deliberately embarrass Europeans.

In general it would not embarrass a mixed-race person for it to be known in his community that he associates with Europeans, but if he overdoes it or boasts about it, he is disliked. In general there is no great in-group pressure to confine interaction to those of mixed race and exclude either Europeans, Papuans, or New Guineans.

The ability to "pass" has a great influence in the promotion of mixed-race–European interpersonal relationships. Mixed-race persons whose physical and cultural attributes allow them to pass are disliked by others of mixed race, who regard them as snobbish. One married mixed-race couple of light skin color whose first child was also light experienced a reduction in the frequency of their interactions with European acquaintances after a second, dark, child was born. A member of the upper class had pointed out differences between mixed-race–European relationships in Lae and Port Moresby, owing, in his view, to the more favorable housing situation in Lae, which is situated on the north side of the island. The formation of subgroups along racial lines in hotel bars has also been observed in Port Moresby though not in Lae.

The character of the relationship between European employer and mixed-race employee has a bearing in the success of the enterprise and the contributions made by both parties. One unsuccessful European employer, who has struggled for fifteen years and who has had twenty-three mixed-race employees at various times, considered them reliable "in front of your face, no good behind," irregular in attendance and erratic in performance, irresponsible and at times dishonest. On the other hand, a company director with thirty years' experience in employing persons of mixed race considered them good foremen or supervisors, whose so-called unreliability resulted from having nothing to bind them to the society, nothing to aspire to, and always having been in poor circumstances. They always requested separate accommodations, each preferring his own cottage. He had found them adaptable, being the first of the local people to learn to drive cars and become motor mechanics. He pointed out the higher frequency of interaction between Europeans and persons of mixed race in Samarai, where officials, business people, and those of mixed race are seen together at social functions, and he noted that the limited mixing in Port Moresby was due to lack of common interests. No company functions were attended by mixed-race persons in Port Moresby.

In reviewing his early life, one upper-class man reported that some missionaries, nuns, and teachers regarded mixed-race people as natives—that is, of equal low status in the total society. Some wished them to remain in *laplaps* (waistcloths), and one said, "You are no better than natives!" This man claims that he was told at school, "Take off your shoes and socks; you can't wear them here!" During that period it was an advantage to have had a European father. Such children received preferential treatment from both Papuan school children and European teachers.

Formerly Europeans were not spontaneously invited into mixed-race homes. They were met with, "Don't come in, this is a funny old place!" An upper-class mixed-race person who was transported home on many occasions by a European friend failed to invite the European in until a request was made.

In April 1961, in what is believed to be the first case of its kind in the country, a mixed-race woman was awarded $1,000 in damages in the Port Moresby Supreme Court against a European for breach of promise to marry. She claimed over-all damages of $10,000, including loss of wages at $75 per month. The Judge found that the defendant had promised to marry her in December 1959 and had been a constant visitor to her home from December 1959 to February 1960.

Papuans show little overt hostility to those of mixed race. A broad spectrum of relationships is to be observed. The unsophisticated and uneducated Papuan has little interest in or awareness of mixed-race society. In interview he tends to classify mixed-race people as being of his own kind (as different from Europeans or Chinese), and he usually interacts fairly freely with them. On the other hand, educated Papuans have given the matter more thought. The few who have traveled widely within the country have commented on the varying character of mixed-race–Papuan interrelationships in the different towns. Some say that the mixed-race people in New Britain are much disliked by the Tolais, toward whom they have adopted superior attitudes, and they feel that circumstances are better in Port Moresby. Others say that mixed-race people and Papuans in Port Moresby show mutual distaste, as in the nurse-patient relationship in the hospital setting. Still others say that they are content for those of mixed race to stay when independence comes, provided they pay their taxes and cause no trouble. In the Koke-Badili area, where there are all shades of skin color from jet black to café au lait, mixed-race–indigenous tensions are not conspicuous.

Among the Papuan and New Guinean relatives of mixed-race people, two groups stand out: those who accept the mixed-race people as themselves and those who attach considerable significance to non-Papuan ancestry and thereby concede a superiority in status. Whereas a Papuan feels no such superordinate-subordinate relationship with his own relatives, formerly he would not walk into a mixed-race house without asking permission. Papuan relatives of mixed-race people are mostly very affectionate toward them. On meeting after some time they may be overdemonstrative, apply cheek to cheek, and breathe in deeply, and the mixed-race person may feel embarrassed should a European be present. One exception to this is the acculturated Hanuabadan, whose relationship to his mixed-race relatives and friends is more formal. Where, however, it is a matter of exchange of indigenous goods, there is noticeable generosity on both sides.

Mixed-race social-class divisions are based on the tendency to absorb European values and the capacities of individuals to adapt to pressures deriving from these tendencies. Those with greater capacity show a marked desire to detach themselves from the less happily endowed, with a resultant crystallization of an upper-class group. Certain persons eat, drink, play and interact together in various ways to the exclusion of others. The lower ranks tend to group on the basis of denial or by identification with prevailing Papuan values, except when threatened with classification as Papuans. There is thus an attraction towards both ends of the scale, with a larger group remaining in the middle. This triad of upper, middle, and lower social classes within the mixed-race community reflects that of the larger pre-Independence social structure, with its Caucasian upper class, mixed-race middle class, and Papuan lower class. These subdivisions are not permanent but indicate those who tend to be social and organizational equals. Upper-class mixed-race people are either in private enterprise or the professions, middle-class people are artisans, and those in the lower class are unskilled laborers or unemployed.

There are other lesser indices which do not relate directly to status but which are associated with membership in a given class—for example, the so-called "chee chee" accent is normally absent in upper-class mixed-race women but readily returns under stress, when they revert to the language of their childhood, which was influenced by French nuns, French missionaries, and Papuan non-English-speaking children.

Other features associated with membership in a given class include the following:

1. *Upper class.* These people, also known as the "top class," are described by other mixed-race people with such phrases as, "They are distinct because they let you know it"; "Everyone acknowledges it"; "They wouldn't invite anyone from Gabutu"; "Nobody would dare invite them to a beer party at Gabutu"; "Their daughters are waiting for better-type husbands."

The interiors of their homes resemble those of Europeans, though they are less elaborate. The women insist on curtains in their houses but prefer wood stoves. Most possess table napkins, but they are seldom used except for a "distinguished visitor," usually the parish priest or a European. Cutlery and kitchenware equal that in Port Moresby European homes. Table cloths are used at all times. Wine is served with dinner when guests are present and is drunk in moderation.

These people are conscious of fashion, but because of limited incomes some of their clothing is out of date by European standards. A woman might own, for example, one modern and seven old-fashioned dresses, a ratio often reversed for European women of Port Moresby. Permanent wave hair styles are confined to this class. The women attend church less frequently than those in the lower classes and do not play "lucky." Most men own tuxedos, and all have a few neckties. In 1956, "whites" and shark-skin clothing were worn by Europeans and upper- and middle-class mixed-race men, but with Europeans now wearing terylene and the like, mixed-race men are often unable to keep up. Pajamas and nightgowns are worn.

Upper-class mixed-race people may complain of "too much family," and daughters are urged to maximize their status by marriage with such warnings as, "You don't want to carry a *kiapa* bag on your head all your life!" The existence of bridewealth is stoutly denied.

2. *Middle class*. These people, also known as the "artisan class," do tradesmen's jobs, in 1963 received wages between $80 and $100 per month, and retained their class position almost solely by virtue of their seniority with the administration.

In their homes, family portraits are displayed. Wall paint is rare or, if present, is unrelated to a color scheme. Furniture is usually old and purchased second hand. A wood stove is preferred, but occasionally a primus stove is used.

Not everyone owns a bed, and some sleep on a mattress on the floor. The baby hammock is prominent. Tablecloths are rarely used, although they may appear for upper-class mixed-race visitors. Knives and forks are used in the American way, with food being first cut with a knife and then eaten with a fork or spoon in the right hand. As with the other two classes, the children use spoons only until they reach adulthood, after which they adopt the patterns of the particular class they enter. Crockery is sparse and aluminum ware predominates. Soup plates and sweet dishes are not used. Meals consist of one course only, and food is placed on the table in a bowl from which each person serves himself.

The women wear plain but quite attractive dresses, brassieres, and shoes. Most mothers, however, wear shoes only into town. Before the war, with the exception of the upper class, very few wore shoes at all. There is a fashion lag of three or four years with respect to women's dresses. This class is not fashion-conscious, but mothers are proud to point out that their children are sent to school well dressed, and some boast about giving one dollar per week to the teaching sisters at Koke so that their children get a prestige lunch. Pajamas and nightgowns are not worn, and women generally sleep in their petticoats.

These people are somewhat restrained in arrangements for their parties. Invitation cards are printed, and they are delivered by hand, as there is no postal delivery service in Port Moresby. They claim to "invite everyone," but some upper-class mixed-race people insist that they would never dream of attending such parties.

The quasi matriarch or *booboo* is most prevalent in this class. She is the oldest woman and exercises considerable power over her children and grandchildren. Her function is regulatory in that she can readily bring dissident young women into line with such a devastating and oblique reference to legitimacy as, "You came off the grass!"

3. *Lower class*. These people are sometimes referred to as the "booze parties class" because of their frequent drinking parties. Their homes are simple, often with walls of old corrugated iron. Furniture and shelves are improvised from packing cases. There is normally a table, but they usually eat and sleep on the floor. The ubiquitous baby hammock is permanently tied to the rafters with a piece of rope.

Food is usually taken with the fingers and each person helps himself. Enamel plates and cups, some aluminum dishes, and spoons are used. The typical stove is made from half a forty-four-gallon drum with a hole cut in the side, and either holes punched in the top or a wire mesh top. Alternatively, two metal pipes across two wooden blocks may be used for cooking.

The women are not fashion-conscious, and few possess shoes or brassieres. They make their own clothing but are not skilled in style or fit. The men may wear *laplaps* and the women dresses for sleeping.

They are often mistaken for Papuans by Europeans but never by other mixed-race people. All are conscious of the hazard of being incorrectly classified as Papuans, and formerly they feared losing the acquisitions which went with mixed-race status. Some endeavored to rectify this by a chance of residence—from Hanuabada to Hohola, for example. Sorcery beliefs are common among members of this group who, if sick, will seek out the Papuan *babalau* as well as the European medical practitioner.

Status among these people is determined principally by occupational and racial criteria. The Caucasian component of the mixture is greatest in the upper, and least in the lower class. The whiter the individual, the easier the expression of the preferred European values.

Although the mixed-race woman ultimately determines the level and style of life within the family, by bringing her husband down or up to her level, her social class is deter-

mined mainly by residence and her husband's employment. Mixed-race men who have been to Australia, and
who may have had a secondary education, often tend to
slide back on marrying a lower-class mixed-race woman
when they return. In some cases such persons have become heavy-equipment operators, a name about which
they boast but which does not impress their peers. Lower-
or middle-class men who marry higher in the social scale
endeavor to adhere to the new standards; yet they sometimes pine for what they refer to as the good old days,
regretting the loss of former friends though not actively
seeking their continued association. The exception to this
is the upper-class spinster whose occupational status
equals her class membership, since she is not usually associated with close family life and lives on her own.

The highest male occupational status is assigned to professionals and businessmen, then plantation owners and
managers, artisans of all kinds, clerks, truck drivers,
stevedores, heavy-equipment operators and casual laborers in that order. The last two have a self-image higher than
that accorded to them by others. Artisans predominate.
Dislike of discipline is widespread, but few engage in
private enterprise on their own. One mixed-race man endeavored to establish himself as a trade-store operator, but
he soon lost all his money. The professional men claim in
some contexts not to mix with the mixed-race community,
but in others they complain of "too much family" and are
well versed in their activities and personalities. The two
attitudes are not, of course, mutually exclusive. Employment with the government is highly prized.

The highest female occupational status is assigned to the
nursing sister, then comes the nursing trainee, nursing
aide, casual baby sitter, telephonist, shop assistant,
dressmaker, bakery assistant, and housewife in that order.
The occupations of nurse, telephonist, and casual baby
sitter bring the aspiring mixed-race woman into contact
with facets of European behavior. She models her home

and family on what she can learn through these sources.

The highly romantic coloration of courtship characteristic of European couples does not apply in Port Moresby mixed-blood society. Girls and youths meet at milk bars, parties, and dances. The explorative "getting acquainted" situation par excellence, however, is the "after the dance" period. There is very little of the pattern of the boy going to the father of the girl and asking to take her out. The young people meet in a surreptitious fashion until their association is public knowledge. If the father of the girl then approves, it will continue more openly. If not, he will put a temporary stop to it by forbidding his daughter to go out. He is usually worn down by persistence or pregnancy. Formal engagement is an institution whose existence varies with social class. When present, as it is among the upper class, the boy usually provides the girl with an engagement ring, for which he will pay in the vicinity of two to four American dollars. There is usually a party of celebration, which is held at the home of the more prosperous parents. It is a big affair with pig, chicken, deer, and wallabies. Both families will have representatives who go hunting prior to the party and who vie with one another in bringing in the biggest catch. As on other mixed-blood social occasions, the party goes on all day, all night, and the next day. There is also much drinking.

Mixed-race people state that prewar courtships usually lasted around six months. In the case of a girl in a convent and a boy outside, the courtship may last up to eighteen months (in one instance, four years) since they do not get together as often as they would like. The girls are learning either domestic science or nursing and are permitted only one or two nights out per week. Normally the girl has to finish her course, and the older ones say that courting was actively discouraged for this reason. Courtships outside convents are shorter; most girls marry within six months of first acquaintance because they become pregnant.

Mixed-blood–mixed-blood courtship. Many Roman Catholics have their courtships promoted by their elders, both within the church and among their relatives. This form of matchmaking is later regarded with ambivalence: some blame it for marriages that "go on the rocks," while others aver that wisdom was introduced where it had previously been lacking. Others meet at parties and many become pregnant. Upperclass people say that this is caused by a lack of sex education. Partners in these courtships are variously described as going in "batches" and "bunches" to the cinema and having group "necking parties."

Mixed-blood–Australian courtship. The majority of Europeans in this connection are New Australian men—that is, Caucasian migrants from Europe. Eligible European spinsters are much fewer than bachelors, and many are known to have come to Papua New Guinea with a view to maximizing their status through marriage. Men in the lowest social class of Europeans—and this includes the New Australians—are thus at a disadvantage in seeking mates within their own racial group. Elderly mixed-race people report that New Australians ask them, "Can I go out with a mixed-race girl?" and "Will I get into trouble with the authorities?"

Mixed-blood–Papuan courtship. Although many courtships result in more or less permanent liaisons, most are not validated by legal marriage. Until recently, very few Papuans came to mixed-race parties. Mixed-race people now also go to Papuan parties. Courting between mixed-race girls and Papuan youths is rare, however. Mixed-race youths meet Papuan girls at native functions—a dance at Hanuabada or Kaugere, for example, where there are string bands and European type dances. Most pairs usually elope, since the youth wishes to avoid paying a bride price. Very few mixed-race boys are married to Hanuabadan girls because of the high bride price, which may be

$1,000 or more and in some instances reaches $4,000. A mixed-race–Papuan courtship more usually results in marriage when the boy meets the girl out of town—in a coastal village, for example, and brings her back to Port Moresby. In all such cases known to me they have eloped. The District Office will ask the youth whether he wants to marry by European or Papuan custom. He is usually in a poorly paid position, and if he should marry by Papuan custom, he might never stop paying bride price. The mixed-race youth who wishes to marry a Papuan is usually unable to attract a mixed-race girl.

In other cases propinquity is important. A mixed-race man may wish to marry a Papuan girl who went to the same mission school. She is acceptable in mixed-race society because the couple have educational standards, religion, and other interests in common. Such courtships may be fostered, and subsequent marriage considered highly successful. In many marriages between mixed-race men and indigenous women, the social customs of the woman prevail. If such practices as eating on the floor are adopted, upper-class mixed-race relatives and friends express distaste.

The bridewealth practice, designed to stabilize marital unions in nonliterate societies, is surprisingly widespread among mixed-race people, although the compensatory function (for loss of a valued asset) seems more prominent here. Bridewealth is found in all three social classes, although there is a tendency to deny its existence. Negotiations are described as being conducted "under the hat," as few wish to be identified with Papuans. In Gabutu, prices of $400 and $800 are known to have been paid in this fashion. One Australian married to a mixed-race girl received many indirect hints which he successfully resisted, as he was already supporting some of his wife's relatives. The concept of bride price is sometimes easier for New Australians to absorb, and one continental European married to a middle-class mixed-race woman said that as the dowry system was operative in his country, he did not find the idea of bride price unusual and readily paid it. A lower-class mixed-race man who had paid a bride price of $160 and who passed all the tests for mixed-race status as herein defined found himself classified by a magistrate as a "native" under the Liquor Ordinance because he had paid bride price and lived in Hanuabada village without a permit, although he knew a permit to be necessary for nonindigenes. An upper-class mixed-race girl, whose bride price was known to be $2,000, attempted to elope with a Papuan, to the consternation of her kinsfolk. She was retrieved and confined to the house.

Mixed-blood–mixed-blood marriages. There were no divorces and only two separations. One was a marriage arranged by the mission, and there was gross disparity in intelligence and personal tastes, aggravated by poor housing. Where the homes are inadequate, some of the women do not care to clean them. There may be no food available when the husband comes home, so he may go off to drink. There seem to be few special problems with the younger children of these marriages, but the teenagers drink, gamble, and have sexual experience at an early age. The pattern is modeled on that of the parents; for example, one teenage party lasted for three days. By and large, however, marriage is stable.

Mixed-blood–Australian marriage. Most are stable in the sense that they persist. Disharmony, however, is common. Interests and intellectual standards are not the same except in the case of the few better-educated mixed-race girls recently returned from Australia. The first six months are reasonably harmonious; then the man may realize that he and his wife do not have the same interests. An important reintegrating factor is rejection by European society. Also, most of these European husbands are in an anomic position in relation to their own culture, and many readily admit to religious agnosticism. Nevertheless, married couples under these circumstances lack common ground for discussion. They cannot discuss Australian politics or horse racing, subjects which interest many such men, or the local issues which interest the women. Some men who bring their friends home dislike having their wives bring theirs.

Mixed-blood–Papuan customary marriage. Most are between mixed-race men and Papuan women, although in seven cases mixed-race women had married Papuan men. The former fall into two groups, those that break up and those where the mores of the Papuan partner are adopted. The mixed-race men concerned have minimal standards of living and would not readily attract mixed-race girls. In marriages of mixed-race women to Papuan men the man makes every effort to maintain the standard of living to which his wife has been accustomed. He is usually proud of his high-class marriage. In both instances the woman is an important determiner of standards.

The least fortunate children in Port Moresby are those of mixed race, most of whose parents have little in the way of cultural patterns and mores to govern their behavior. From their earliest years they have incomplete access to the broader culture of the area. Social instability and a comparatively poor economic position are transmitted to the offspring. Families are often split on the basis of skin coloration, and darker children remain in the background when Europeans visit. There is also a great difference between children and teenagers. Prepubertal social life is not directed so much by internal physiological drives as by environmental stimuli, and the children reproduce the activities of their elders as far as possible.

During the first five years the child appears completely happy. There is no discipline and little routine. He is happy because of the companionship of many people. He goes to bed (usually on a mat on the floor) only when he wants to. After that age he is at a disadvantage because of his father's frequent absences and his mother's lack of foresight. For example, mothers may not give their children money, may not prepare their lunches, or may have no food in the house. Gabutu children going for a school examination one afternoon had had neither breakfast nor lunch, according to one teacher.

The child first tends to become conscious of himself as a mixed-race person when he goes to school. He becomes quiet, and this accounts for the so-called "good behavior" of mixed-race children. He soon recognizes his intermediate position in the social structure by minor acts of discrimination by his elders, such as, for example, being made by the teacher to give up his seat in a bus for a European child. Those with European fathers are noticeably more lively, but the darker ones tend to hold back. Parents do not seem to use punishment as much as European parents do, indifference being more marked among the middle and lower classes. Another important conditioning experience is provided where the father comes home from work and tells his wife of some difficulty with a European; this atmosphere is readily absorbed by the child.

Much of the attention given by mothers to their children is practical. Many spend a large amount of time gambling, but it is rarely acknowledged as such, and the rest of the time they spend in washing, in nursing, and in domestic chores. Only a few of the upper class spend any time playing with, reading stories to, or talking to their children.

Women's social club meetings are carried on regardless of the presence of children, who always outnumber the mothers. The mothers' attitude is permissive. The children are well dressed, but none wear shoes. They crawl on the floor and play quietly with one another, and their presence can be readily forgotten. There is no "showing off" or the noisy behavior so often a feature of comparable European gatherings.

Upper-class parents say that their children learn more quickly than Papuan and less quickly than European children. Most consider this a result of the environment out of school. They point out that whereas six years ago mixed-race children were in the sixth grade at sixteen years of age, today they are in the same grade at thirteen. They anticipate that the same standard will soon be achieved at eleven to twelve years of age. Educating and caring for mixed-race children have been undertaken mainly by the Roman Catholic missions and to a lesser extent by other missions. Nowadays there is no segregation and the framework exists for equality of opportunity, at least in theory. Formerly the Roman Catholic mission conducted two schools at Port Moresby in the villages of Hanuabada and Bomana. The latter has recently been closed. Mixed-race children made up half the pupil population at these schools, the other half being Papuan. The education given at these schools was equivalent to that offered in Papuan schools and compared unfavorably with that gained by mixed-race teenagers in Australia. (Financial assistance for secondary schooling in Australia was arranged in 1956, pending the introduction of secondary schools in Papua New Guinea for all races.)

School attendance is irregular. The smallest difficulty will result in mixed-race children's staying away. Physical illness is sometimes responsible, although in general these children are notoriously healthy. Children may not have enough change of clothes, especially in the wet season, or their clothes may not have been ironed. Parents will keep children at home rather than send them to school ill clad. Clothes as a status symbol take precedence over the long-range values of education. Cases are known in which parents have kept children away from school for months following minor accidents in order to promote their chances of obtaining legal damages.

Lower-class women usually have their children in their arms whenever they are not in the house. The child is held in all positions, including astride the hip, and is lifted out of a vehicle by the wrist only, rather than in the safer fashion of being lifted under the shoulders with both hands. The child accepts this without demurring. These women suckle their children in the street without embarrassment.

As do their parents, these children hate discipline. They commonly run away from school. Very few have joined the Boy Scouts, Cubs, or Brownies. Some join, but they soon withdraw. Many do not like mixing with Papuans if they can avoid it, particularly if they might be surpassed.

Religion plays a large part in their upbringing, and they are baptized at an early age. Most parents are strong Roman Catholics and make their children say their prayers as soon as they can talk. Even before this they are shown the sign of the cross and religious pictures on the wall. Their religious education begins earlier than does that of European children. Much of what they do is related to religion. Commonly heard are such phrases as, "You mustn't do so and so, it is a sin," and "You must do so and so for the souls in purgatory." This practice is much stronger among the lower than among the middle and upper classes.

As the child grows up, supervision falls away. The parent has no control whatsoever over children from the ages of twelve to fourteen. As boys grow older, they develop a wider appreciation of their parents and the environment in which they live. These changes begin at eight to nine years of age in boys and a little later in girls. Parental loss of control then continues, and it explodes at puberty. Because children are being educated better than their parents were, they resent being told what to do. One often hears such phrases as, "Shut up, you old bitch!" and "Take no notice of him, he's an old bastard!" Older mixed-race people refer nostalgically to prewar days, when this was just not done, they say. Nowadays adolescents will exchange blows with their parents. They also insist that parents continue to look after them when they have grown up. Very few pay board. Some say that they occasionally "toss Mum a dollar." Very few parents chase the dissident children out of the home.

Among the males, the drinking of alcoholic beverages is almost universal. Along with gambling it is the distinguishing feature of the cultural life of the people. Persons of mixed race used to avoid one hotel, saying that the management was snobbish, because they asked to see liquor permits even when the mixed-race customer was known, in order to imply that he was not wanted. Some lighter-skinned mixed-race persons went there, they say, not because they preferred it, but because it was more convenient. A second hotel was patronized freely, but one could not walk into it comfortably wearing overalls, and there was a tendency to segregate European and mixed-race persons. Most use was made of a section of a third hotel which was formerly an old copra shed. One had to pass down some steps to reach it. It had an atmosphere of basement exclusiveness, and mixed-race persons expressed a feeling of security and identity there, saying that they felt themselves to be intruders in the bars patronized mainly by Europeans. It was frequented principally by mixed-race people and working-class Europeans, with a small percentage of upper-class Europeans. The latter, according to the mixed-race people, considered themselves "tough" by patronizing this bar.

The second most important context of drinking is the party. A few years ago a number of Europeans attended mixed-race drinking parties, but by 1962 they were almost exclusively confined to mixed-race people. One meets another in the street and says, "We're having a party" or "We're putting on a show." A "reason" or "purpose" is always given—for example, one's wife's birthday or a child's birthday. Guests are offered drinks on arrival, but they will also have had something to drink before arriving.

Parties start at about eight in the evening with music and dancing. There may be something to eat, but food is secondary: the emphasis is on drinking, which goes on all night, and often all the next day as well. There is usually a fight. Mixed-race men say, "There must be a fight or it is not a party," or "It is more or less expected and accepted." Methods of precipitating a fight take the following forms. A man may make a nuisance of himself by singing too much, another might talk too much, or a third may slap too heartily the back of one he normally dislikes. Many are described as having a "chip on the shoulder," and requiring very little to set them off. Not infrequently a man is riled by the thought that another may be better than he in some particular way, and he may go the party deliberately seeking a fight. One man at a party informed me that he was challenged at almost every one he attended. After the party all may be good friends again. Informants frequently reiterate that they have been brought up to think they belong to a class who are "in the background." They indicate that this has constantly been made clear to them through the behavior-patterning agencies of parents, peers, teachers, and social structure. Their own comments are, "The only time a mixed-race person feels superior is when he has a few beers in him," and "He wants to prove that he is equal to the next." Hence, as with gambling, and in this instance through the medium of the drunken fight, fate is asked to speak in favor of the individual.

Drinking is less prominent and less frequent at picnics and cricket matches. Teenagers, however, are often seen piling bottles into battered old second-hand cars and tearing off into the night. In the eyes of mixed-race youths, drinking is manly. "It's great!" Solitary drinkers and "secret" drinkers of the type existing in Australian communities are not found, although a man may sometimes drink in short-term solitude when having a "hate session" against another member of the group.

After-work hotel drinking and drinking parties can be

looked upon as social rituals, performed both because they symbolize social solidarity and because they promote interpersonal relationships, even if sometimes only in a negative or hostile sense. The tensions and anxieties almost always present in a mixed-race person's sober state are often resolved under the influence of alcohol in these situations. Normally painful interactions are then handled with comfort. Drinking promotes interpersonal performance in all directions, including interactions across caste barriers. The latter are not always favorable, however, for it is in just such a situation that a mixed-race person's resentment of Europeans finds overt expression in the presence of Europeans. Aggression and violence in some instances take precedence over mellowness.

Drinking and drunkenness are highly prized among the men. To most, particularly in the lower and middle classes, it is considered a sine qua non to any joy in life, and it is also thought to have health-giving properties. The majority of mixed-race women, however, do not drink. They are chiefly concerned with the financial side of the men's drinking, which may take up to two-thirds or three-quarters of their salary. The women castigate their husbands frequently but not always with circumspection, as is evidenced by the regular appearance of black eyes among the women. Prudence dictates caution in an explosive situation, and subtle methods are employed indirectly through the children, who are guided to side with the mother. A husband may stay away for several days on a "grogging spree," and the children may say, "Daddy, you drink too much," or "I know where you're going." It is common to hear children talking this way, but quite useless, as father "carries on, regardless."

Alcohol has been readily available at any store, and the mixed-race community has had drinking rights since 1956. The most popular drinks, in order, are beer, port wine, rum, and gin. Little direct pressure is applied to young people to follow this pattern, but they readily do so in imitation of their elders.

In his sober state, the mixed-race person is generally shy and retiring in the company of Europeans; many say he is afflicted with an inferiority complex, which hounds him from birth and ceases only with death. The person of mixed race is constantly preoccupied with what others think of him, and with "the way we are treated." He has great sensitivity to hurt and is skilled in preserving the feelings of others, because he dislikes being hurt himself. He does not always exercise this skill, however. When he becomes drunk, this withdrawn state disappears; he becomes loquacious, noisy, repetitious, and aggressive, and he actively seeks someone to fight. This is not difficult, as many others are in the same state. With the return of sobriety, the withdrawn attitude in the presence of Europeans reappears, and friendliness is resumed with other mixed-race people.

In hotels, the odd member who feels that he has had enough is subjected to such phrases as: "Can't you take it?", "You're weak," "Frightened of your missus?" and "Man or mouse?" At parties, too, it is difficult to refuse a drink. Not refusing is perhaps the most important drinking rule. Soft drinks are frowned upon. All must bring their share of alcohol to a party. Anyone seen transgressing the drinking rule by pouring a drink out the window will have his glass filled up, and he will be stood over until it is empty.

Some Europeans think that the mixed-race people drink too much and ask, "How can they afford to drink?" In their view, if a person earns less he should drink less, but there is little active malice on the part of Europeans. Such prejudice and discrimination as there is confines itself largely to expressions of dislike of mixed-race drinking or the behavior of mixed-race persons while drunk.

Most Papuans questioned did not express views on

mixed-race drinking, though the more sophisticated re-
sented it. They said, "What's so special about him? He's no
different from us." Some made a distinction in this connection between persons whom they called "proper half-
caste" (that is, having some European ancestry), whose
drinking they didn't mind, and those with no European
ancestry (for example, a person of Samoan-Papuan ancestry), who, they said, should not have been allowed to
drink.

Drinking is a social matter in the mixed-race society of
Port Moresby and plays an important part in the function-
ing of the group, whose members are made up of indi-
vidualists. Although it serves personal needs, the primary
purpose is to meet the expectations of the group. This is
illustrated by the absence of pathological drinking, as opposed to "hard drinking." The mixed-race person's desire
for social participation was also shown by circumstances in
the earlier period under which many "supplied liquor to
natives illegally." The socioeconomic basis of this widespread activity was made clear to me by the fact that I
became aware of only three persons of mixed-race who did
it solely for economic reasons. The majority bought and
supplied liquor without a profit to share with Papuan relatives or friends. Some went to jail for this offense, then
returned and did it again. One mixed-race man went to jail
three times, for six months on each occasion, for the same
offense. A further illustration is provided by the act of
simulating drunkenness. A sober man who has had nothing to drink will often stagger about and pretend to be
drunk on entering the group situation. Should a fight
develop, the "drunkenness" is instantly abandoned.

Alcoholic addiction and alcoholic mental disorders are
unknown among these people. General and mental hospital records do not provide any account of such cases, something that cannot be said of the other drinking group, the
Europeans, despite the fact that the latter claim that they

drink with circumspection and that persons of mixed race do not. As has been indicated above, drinking by the mixed-race people is primarily confined to social contexts and only secondarily to the handling of individual interpersonal problems.

The small upper class show considerable restraint in drinking, which is chiefly with meals. They keep good wines, whisky and crème de mentho for their visitors. Sherry is offered before dinner.

The middle class are more likely to invite all who will come and bring alcohol with them to their parties, and they openly remind guests "You must bring some grog." They are still somewhat restrained in that invitation cards are often sent, parties occur only about twice a year for each family, and a special occasion is used as a pretext—a daughter may have just started (or finished) school, for example. At the beginning of these parties, the convenor asks everyone to behave himself, saying that he doesn't want the police to visit. Nevertheless, the parties frequently end in fights and broken furniture.

Members of the lower class exhibit no restraint. In their own phrase, they put on a drinking party "at the drop of a hat," or as soon as they have a few dollars. They invite everyone, saying, "Bring your own grog." Almost every night there is one going on somewhere, most frequently in Gabutu.

Gambling is the other characteristic activity of the mixed-race people and is indulged in freely by men, women, and children alike. "Lucky" was introduced into Port Moresby during the Second World War, according to the older mixed-race people, before which the principal game was one called "In and Out," which is now extinct. Lucky is illegal, and there are police raids occasionally. Somebody initiates a game, which is then held regularly at his or her place for several months until it becomes well known and is raided by the police. Then the site is shifted.

The householder has no special powers relevant to the game. He is responsible for the venue only. A "cockatoo" is assigned the task of announcing the approach of the police to insure rapid dispersal. The big games commence on pay night and may last three days. Lucky may be played on a lawn, on a verandah, under a tree, or on a beach, but mostly it is on the floor of a house, on a mat or blanket. The players eat and sleep there; meals are brought along by their families. Not much is eaten during the game, but there may be a pause for food. Sometimes whole families will play.

The continuity of the game is insured by the institutionalized system of borrowing. If a person loses he will borrow from within one circle, and the game will go on and on. Most borrowing is done during the game. Sometimes a person may bet on credit. This is not liked but may be tolerated for two or three rounds. When the borrower wins agains, he has to pay back what he owes. In the process of borrowing, the borrower does not usually ask; he just takes the money and says, "I'll owe you that!" The lender may protest, but not greatly. This type of borrowing keeps the game going for days. If one wants to leave the game earlier, one will be taunted as a piker or a coward or as wanting something for nothing. He is regarded as one who is not doing his share and is running away from group obligations. Port Moresby mixed-race gamblers qua gamblers are good friends in the borrowing context—not in the sense of being bosom pals, but because they understand each other's needs. Such emphatic interactions have a functional purpose. Lenders may grumble but do not usually refuse. On rare occasions a gambler may borrow from relatives after a game, but this cannot persist, as they become disillusioned. Sometimes credit can be obtained from trade stores for maintenance during a losing period, but this too has it limitations and cannot persist. In short, survival of the pool as a group is dependent upon borrowing within the gambling group.

In big pay-weekend games of lucky, amounts of $600 or $800 may be circulating at any one time, which are considerable amounts by mixed-race standards. Sometimes Papuans join these games, but it is rare for Europeans to be associated. When it is exclusively a mixed-race game, the total numbers present may not exceed sixteen or seventeen. When others are invited, there may be as many as forty persons. As there are only fifty-two cards in the pack, and each person has three cards, the inner ring of actual players consists of sixteen or seventeen persons (except in the very rare instances when two packs of cards are used). The average number is ten to fifteen. The outer ring has about twenty-three or twenty-four nonplayers who bet on individual inner-ring players' cards.

The inner-ring players are the real gamblers. They bet on their own cards and take side bets with the persons next to them. The outer-ring players are bettors and watchers. They may not put money in the center unless they become inner-ring players. They are mobile and bet on anyone's cards with anyone. Cards are dealt clockwise, and the deal passes clockwise among the players. The pack is cut by the person who dealt the preceding hand, and each player is dealt three cards. The highest number over ten or better (for example, the highest of three of a kind) wins. The bet is made before the player sees his cards. The dealer deals to himself first, the cards go round, and everyone looks. The bets may be, for example, fifty cents each, and all bets are placed in the center. The winner takes the lot. There are side bets by mutual arrangement. Anyone can "call the tune" (that is, the size of the bet). He says, for example, "Two dollars center," and another not yet prepared to go so far may say, "Make it a dollar." A majority decision determines the amount in the center, and others have to be satisifed with side bets if they cannot meet it. The size of a side bet is by mutual arrangement. When his luck is going well, a player will extend his operations and may have three or four side bets at once. A side bet in the outer ring can sometimes amount to more than that of the individual bet in the inner ring; the amount of money in the center is more, however. The individual member of the inner ring will not as a rule bet on cards other than his own. He may, of course, have side bets in this connection.

The game becomes heated when individual players start losing. Each hopes to win money quickly, and if he or she does not, he goes home to an inevitable row with the spouse. It is possible to lose a fortnight's wages within a couple of hours. This is a source of much domestic dishar-mony, particularly when the spouse is a nongambler. Usu-ally about one-third of the players in these weekend games are women, and they are distributed fairly equally be-tween the inner- and outer-ring groups. They also play every day. There is an average of ten regulars in this female pool. Fighting breaks out among the women on occasions associated with real or assumed transgressions by other players.

Though lucky involves no skill, most of the other gambl-ing games do. It seems then, that where the aleatory ele-ment is greatest, there the mixed-race person would be, buffered as he is on both sides by two larger groups to neither of which he is acceptable. As with other areas of his social life, magical beliefs play a prominent part in his thinking. In an attempt to control the chance element, he may believe that a pregnant woman has more luck, and she is sent out to gamble while her husband stays at home to "mind the kids." He may believe that certain foods are unlucky when gambling, that the evil thoughts of others are unlucky, and that it is necessary to carry lucky charms to introduce an element of control. Examples of the latter include a diseased tooth, the supposed teeth of an American airman named Taylor who crashed during the war (the gambler would say, "Come on, Taylor!"), the bark of a special tree, and an ordinary hair comb. When he thinks he is losing at lucky, he will have an exclusive side bet because he associates such a thing with greater luck.

The community attitude towards gambling is that it is "a bad thing." Most mixed-race people say they are against it, but most participate in it. Ex post facto justifications take the form of, "It's better than drinking" and "It's the lesser of two evils." Women, particularly, say it is better than drinking. This, of course, has to be considered against a background in which many of the women drink much less than the men but gamble more.

The mixed-race gambler is ostracized by the mixed-race nongambler, not because of any intrinsic distaste for gambling, as this activity fits the needs of these people well, but rather because of its effect on his efficiency as an economic provider. Mixed-race women who do not gamble (and they are few) say that their husbands' gambling is the cause of all their troubles. Mixed-race men who do not gamble (and they are almost exclusively confined to the upper class) and Europeans say, "How can they afford it?" Some sophisticated Papuans claim that they are not in favor of gambling, but most are not greatly concerned, as they have full access, and gambling, in former times, did not have status-conferring attributes, as drinking rights did.

Gambling rules exist, and there are definite sanctions to deal with transgressions. Gambling debts must be paid on the spot, whatever the circumstances. One meets the situation, if it is necessary, by borrowing within the gambling group. Many forms of dishonesty may be indulged in without too great a loss of face, but the payment of gambling debts is sacred. The structure of the gambling school is based on the premise that the loser will pay his debts.

When one considers that at times $600 to $800 might

change hands in the biggest games, it is not surprising that the atmosphere becomes heated and that arguments ensue. One or two might try to "pull swifties," for example, by not putting their dollars in the center; those who bet on prearranged credit may deny that they owe anything. Some are said to know all the tricks of the trade and, for example, may hide a card up a sleeve. To prevent this from happening, the cards are often counted, and individuals searched. Fist fights sometimes occur as the result of these real or assumed transgressions. Those concerned are pulled apart by the others. Cheats are ideally chased out, but for women, particularly, there is a certain institutionalized evasion of an institutional norm. Women are said to "get up to tricks" more often than the men. If a woman is losing at lucky when both sexes are present, for example, she may lean over and surreptitiously take her fifty cents back, and the men will pretend to ignore it. No man may do this. There is thus a higher threshold of tolerance of the women's behavior by the men in this particular context.

Gambling appears to have existed at all times and in most societies. As a normal feature of social life it produces few damaging effects on the individual or the group, and among the mixed-race people it has important social and recreational functions in an otherwise colorless and spiritless existence. There is the vain hope for status which is expected from large winnings and the attractiveness of the unpredictable and the precarious. For women, the interest is chiefly in the money and the gossip. On occasions of gambling at lucky, middle- and lower-class mixed-race people fuse. Some of the participants would not normally meet each other were it not for the gambling. In this sense it is a social event, like going to a party or a dance. Social distinctions are momentarily forgotten. The participants do not dress up. Men may wear a pair of shorts, a shirt, singlet, and scuffs. They sit on the hard floor, without cushions. They smoke heavily, stubbing their cigarettes on the floor or throwing them out the window. They do not worry about ash trays; occasionally they may use the lid of a tobacco tin. The game is too exciting a business to allow the display of distinctions. The players have a chat beforehand, but once the game has started, everything is serious, and the common emotional interest takes over.

Permanent avoidance of discriminatory situations by passing for white appears to be extremely rare. Port Moresby is too small, and individual members of society are too well known. This surreptitious activity is done more effectively by going to live in another town—Rabaul—for example, or by migrating to Sydney, where one's former status can more readily be hidden. Such behavior is characteristic of some upper-class women who have married European men. Their good education, fair complexion, and minimum of identifying characteristics help to promote their passing under these circumstances. One mixed-race single girl who passed for white in Australia, where she received her education, complained on returning to Port Moresby that she was not getting the same wages as European girls. She stated that in Australia she was treated the same as anybody else, but that in Port Moresby her wages were at mixed-rate rates, $19.50 per week, and that European girls doing exactly the same work were receiving $24.00 per week. She was determined to return to Australia.

Temporary avoidance of discriminatory situations by Papuans passing as mixed-race is more common. Hula girls with straight hair and fair Aroma and Hanuabadan girls readily attempt to pass as mixed-race in order to get mixed-race wages. A tolerant attitude toward this activity is adopted by mixed-race and Papuan people alike; it is looked upon as gaining a justifiable advantage at the European's expense. Some Papuan men attempted to pass as mixed-race to obtain drinking rights in the former prohibition era; in particular, they sought the prestige which could be gained by supplying liquor illegally to Papuan relatives and friends.

Another adaptive, though less common, device is for a mixed-race person—for example, the upper-class mixed-race person whose dark skin color reduces the advantages available to him in mixed-race society—to claim status as a Papuan or New Guinean. He attempts to avoid the penalties of his status by joining the majority, who will become the dominant group when independence comes.

The social character of the mixed-race society of Port Moresby is reflected in the character structure of individual persons. In the presence of whites many are often extremely self-conscious, withdrawn when sober, but hostile when inebriated. Many concede that they have what they refer to as an inferiority complex which dates from first awareness of caste position. The paranoid state is not uncommon, and when associated with some physical disability it is magnified out of all proportion. Ambivalence is the cardinal trait, there is excessive pride in minor achievement, and there is easy discouragement in the face of difficulty. There is little coincidence of interests among individuals.

Stonequist (1937) originally developed the idea that a person on the margin of two cultures is prone to develop certain characteristic features of personality. He laid great stress on ambivalence to the two cultures to which the individual was marginal. Kerckhoff and McCormick (1955; p. 48) list twenty different characteristics which they believe to arise out of the marginal situation, including anxiety, suspicion, aggression, uncertainty, victimization-rejection, and lack of solidarity. In addition, Tumin (1945, p. 261) believes that pain in the presence of his fellows is characteristic of marginal man, and Lewin (1952) suggests that he has an aversion to the less privileged people of his own group. All these features are readily observed among members of Port Moresby mixed-race society. Not greatly stressed as such by these authors, however, and widely present in the group under consideration are what might be termed *visibility skill* and *mixed-race empathy*. *Visibility skill* refers to the capacity to recognize readily who is who in the caste situation, and to place immediately a person in his group whether that group be European, mixed-blood, or indigenous. In the marginal person's mind the borders are well defined, and he is not known to make a mistake in this connection. The nonmarginal European and indigene, however, even with long experience is prone to error and often confuses examples of the high passability upper class mixed-blood with the European, and examples of the educated indigene with the mixed-blood. His image of the boundaries is blurred. *Mixed-race empathy* refers to a warm capacity for projecting himself into the situations and feelings of others. The mixed-blood does not like to be hurt himself, and is therefore acutely aware of, and considerate of the feelings of others, and will readily anticipate their needs in this regard. This marked characteristic would seem to derive from the marginal situation.

The position in 1973 is as follows: Mixed-race marginality is lessening. It would perhaps be too optimistic to expect resolution altogether, but there are forces at work that should do much to limit the trauma. The adoption of stylish clothing of similar type by all races is more extensive than before. The *laplap* and the *rami* have almost disappeared, particularly in the towns. The young people are doing an excellent job, both consciously and unconsciously. They lack much of the bitterness of their forebears and model themselves more on their age peers. Social mixing among the young of all races has markedly increased. The mixed-race people now have houses of better type, some with telephones, and some with curtains inside. These dwellings are replacing former self-constructed ones devoid of any amenities. According to the women, their husbands drink less than before, now that they have a worthwhile place to come home to; and if brawls are an index of this particular assessment, then it is to be noted that they have decreased considerably. On the other hand, gambling is more refractory and seems impervious to the various influences producing the change. There is always the attractiveness of the unpredictable and the precarious. But the over-all improvement is obvious, is commented on by the mixed-race people themselves, and can be attributed, at least in part, to the developing economy consequent upon the introduction of overseas capital, expanding educational opportunities, and modern views on race relations. With the impending independence it is to be hoped that the trend will continue.

6 Papua New Guinea Psychiatry

IN THIS chapter I would like to tell you something about psychiatric practice among nonliterate peoples. I was the first and, during the major portion of the last fifteen years, the sole psychiatrist in the country, responsible for a population of two and a half million people. In the early stages the problems were primarily of an ad ministrative nature, soon to be overshadowed by those of language, custom, and social organization.

Initially the work was carried out under difficult conditions. A small building known as a hospital was erected in a rural setting at Bomana, ten miles from Port Moresby. This consisted of a galvanized-iron shed, an exercise yard, and a storeroom. Rats and other pests did damage to hospital records, so the shed was later abandoned and was subsequently demolished. A new site was then selected on the banks of the Laloki River. This was virgin jungle country with the vegetation in parts so dense that it was often necessary to cut one's way through. A major hazard was the periodic flooding. On one occasion the hospital was under four feet of water. Higher ground was found in the same area which was eventually transformed into what is now the Laloki Psychiatric Center, consisting of a main hospital and a village treatment center. It is an attractive area by local standards and provides a traditional-type atmosphere conducive to the well-being of nonliterate peoples. The system has developed so that today patients are also seen on referral at the newly established Boroko Psychiatric Clinic and Mental Health Headquarters; at the major general hospitals throughout the country, Lae, Rabaul, Madang, Wewak, Goroka, Samarai, and Arawa, as well as smaller rural health centers; and on other field visits throughout all eighteen districts of the country. The cases to which I shall refer do not represent the full range of mental disorder, for some records were lost and on other occasions circumstances were not conducive to the production of adequate histories. They are fully tabulated elsewhere (Burton-Bradley 1973), and I shall confine myself to a descriptive commentary of some of the major categories.

Schizophrenia is the commonest form of serious mental disorder to present itself. Most of the cases do not emerge as well-defined types and are classified as acute or chronic undifferentiated, but a small number can be identified as simple, hebephrenic, catatonic, and paranoid. The diagnosis is complicated by the fact that schizophrenia refers to a group of illnesses, in which the range extends from the slowly developing irreversible cases on the one hand to the short-lived disorders of acute onset and good prognosis on the other. It is further complicated by the beliefs and sentiments of the indigenous people. It is also necessary to differentiate cultural norm from schizophrenic delusion. Nevertheless, many cases stand out when measured against the norms of both patient and doctor. Is the patient's behavior beyond the norms of his own culture, as defined by well-informed kinsmen? And if so, does it correspond with a standard nosological entity of scientific medicine? Oddness or inappropriateness must be odd or inappropriate to members of the patient's own cultural-linguistic group. The criteria that have been employed for establishing the presence of delusion are threefold. The belief must be false in fact, impervious and unshakeable to reasoning and argument, and not accepted by those of the same cultural and social background, that is, by the patient's own kinsmen. Grandiosity and grandiose delusions predominate. Persecutory delusions are less common, and depressive delusions of the type seen in developed societies have not been noted. Schizophrenic hallucinations among the indigenous people tend to persist, a point of some value in the separation of those similar symptoms that arise on a shared cultural basis, and which tend to be of short duration. This Lilliputian content is not uncommon, being derived from the miniature-demon beliefs of some groups.

Incongruity of affect, when present, attracts attention and is rarely confused with any cultural phenomenon. Occasionally what has become known locally as *shame* reaction may simulate this symptom, but the history will usually separate the two. Schizophrenic signs such as withdrawal, catatonia, stupor, and habit deterioration are recognized by their inappropriateness when matched against the cultural group of the patient. A knowledge of the beliefs and customary behaviors of the group in question is mandatory in assessing any symptom thought to be schizophrenic.

In summary, when most or all of such symptoms and signs as thought disorder, affective incongruity, withdrawal from reality, hallucinations, delusions and catatonia are proven in a partially acculturated indigene with a predominantly town rather than village (rural) background, then the diagnosis can reasonably be made. The person of limited cultural contact, the so-called bush individual, rarely presents the symptoms of schizophrenia. This would suggest that the sociocultural influence of the town, with the confusing effect of alien values, may act as a precipitating factor in a predisposed person and give rise to overt schizophrenia. This hypothesis is further supported by the fact that the condition often arises within the first few months of town life and often readily resolves on return to the village.

Reference should be made to what might be referred to as the New Guinea transitory delusional state. Often a young man, usually an intraterritorial migrant to the town, will have a brief episode of agitation and disorientation during which he may be hallucinated and deluded and may commit some aggressive act. The assessment of such a case is vexatious, as the event occurs at night, and by the time he is examined by the psychiatrist the person is usually asymptomatic. Next morning he appears to be perfectly well, both physically and psychologically. A careful history and retrospective appraisal of symptoms is most desirable in view of the forensic importance of the condition and the possible value of this categorization as a defense at law.

Primary mood disorders in their most obvious manifestations take the form of recurrent manic states. The diagnosis is comparatively easy as these seem to be the most culture-free of all the conditions examined. True depressive responses would seem to be uncommon, although depressive equivalents may well be present in what might appear to be primarily psychoneurosis. For differential diagnostic purposes, some reference should be made to *shame* reaction. The distinctive response of the nonliterate person to the real or expected social disapproval of his own kinsmen has had applied to it the label of *shame*. This is the painful emotion associated with subjective awareness that one is likely to be isolated by public criticism and receive punishment. It is a simple, defensive reaction in which the person looks sad, and he may run away or commit suicide. It has certain similarities with the European symptom of depression, but the latter is a different type of compound affect formed by the fusion of such individually simple affects as grief, hurt, grievance, anxiety, and anger, often against a background of discrepancy between aspiration and achievement. Shame considered as a symptom has a different background deriving from the individual's life experiences, is often short-lived, and is revealed in the course of examination when the person is communicative. It usually lacks the prolonged, gloomy, retarded character of some European depressions. The presence or absence of shame in a potentially shame-producing situation, however, is closely related to the social orbit of the individual. He is unlikely to feel shame in relation to his identical transgressions outside his own group.

There has been a tendency to stress the organic factor as the crucial element of primary etiological significance in the pattern of mental disorder in some developing countries, and there is no question that in certain parts of Africa, trypanosomiasis, cerebral malaria, malnutrition, and parasitic infestations have played a large part in the multicausality of mental disorder. By contrast with these countries, cerebral organic syndromes do not appear to play a large part in the totality of abnormal behavior in Papua New Guinea. Patients with cerebral malaria and benign tertian malaria might be clouded in consciousness for brief periods, but even in an endemic malarious area, parasites in the blood have to be demonstrated for the nexus to be established. In the absence of malaria parasites, the significance of the relationship is always open to question. Toxic-infective psychoses arise at times in association with meningitis, both purulent and tuberculous, viral encephalitis, viral hepatitis, pneumonia, and septicemia. Irritability, sometimes associated with mental symptoms and violence, is on occasions associated with the early stages of meningitis. Abnormalities of heat physiology such as heat exhaustion and heat stroke do not appear to be of great importance at the present time. The diagnosis of diabetes is more frequent in urban areas, and psychiatric symptoms are sometimes associated with hypoglycemia. Syphilitic meningoencephalitis is surprisingly rare. Where head injury associated with psychiatric symptoms has been demonstrated, it is most important that the exact time and place of occurrence of the injury are ascertained. It may have occurred before, during, or after any aggressive act that may have taken place. A detailed history and information from other sources will assist in the first two instances, and with the last mentioned, examination may reveal traumatic delirium, posttraumatic personality disorder or deterioration, and psychoneurosis following trauma. Lesser forms of active cerebral disease in predisposed and poorly integrated personalities sometimes precipitate aggressive and other abnormal behavior, but in each case the nexus between the disease process and the actual act in question must be demonstrated.

Unless the doctor himself observes the seizure, great caution is needed in diagnosing epilepsy. Burn scars and amputations in a patient from the colder Highland regions are almost diagnostic. These deformities are the result of the patient's having fallen into a fire during the course of convulsions. Difficulty is sometimes experienced in separating cortical from subcortical cases when it is virtually impossible to establish the age of onset. The patient either cannot remember, or is unable to differentiate a convulsion in his mind from other events such as accidents, sleeping, and fainting, and to communicate this information accurately to others. When there are forensic implications, the mere history of epilepsy does not of itself excuse an alleged offender. Examination may reveal an epileptic equivalent or fugue or postconvulsive confusional state as being more probable than not at the time in question. The court would need to be satisfied that preictal irritability, if present, had impaired a subject's capacity to appraise the wrongfulness of an act.

Taboo transgressions are culture-specific, and a knowledge of the various taboos concerning incest and postpartum sex and of the rules concerning kin avoidance is essential for their correct management. Incest taboos vary considerably among the cultural-linguistic groups. They may be confined to members of the nuclear family and little else, they may include secondary relatives, or, in the case of the Tolais of New Britain, they may involve a person's entire moiety—that is, half the females are by custom unavailable for sexual relations. Transgression of the code may lead to shame and conflict. These rules are tending to break down in many areas, particularly among some of the younger people. Under the present circumstances of rapid social change they are an important source of conflict between father and son and between mother and daughter.

In the indigenous conception of illness, "insanity" and other forms of mental disorder are thought to be due to spirit intrusion within the body, to sorcery, to natural causes, or to no cause at all. Spirit intrusion particularly seems to be related to acute manifestations. Possession syndromes would seem to be less in evidence among educated persons, although along with sorcery symptoms they are perhaps the most resistant to change of all indigenous beliefs. The patient complains of the possession of his body by alien spirits, or two spirits are said to be fighting for access to one body, and there are many other variants of human-spirit interrelationships. These syndromes are associated with marked anxiety, panic, and inability to work. Analysis of the details, empathic understanding of the patient's viewpoint, and environmental manipulation of the attendant circumstances will often bring about a resolution.

Pseudopsychosis is relatively uncommon in European countries, but it is beginning to appear in Papua New Guinea. It is characterized by three things: First, there is a dramatic onset of claimed psychosis associated with a marked desire to enter a state hospital or the psychiatric ward of a general hospital; second, there is a background setting of disparity between the hospital and the home favoring the hospital in terms of food, shelter, and overcrowding; and third, there is a high degree of sophistication in insane and mental-hospital lore. The recognition of this condition is important. Such persons may be admitted to a general hospital for a short period for investigation, but they should not be admitted to a state hospital. They should be sympathetically handled and transferred to social welfare agencies, as it is not in their best interests to be defined as patients.

The custom of betel-nut chewing is well-nigh universal, although less common in remote areas of the highlands. Three fairly well defined syndromes are associated with the practice: betel-nut habituation, betel-nut addiction, and betel-nut psychosis. With habituation a feeling of well-being spreads over the entire body when the nut is chewed. Hunger, tiredness, and irritability disappear. Consciousness remains unimpaired, and there is an increased capacity for work in the hot, humid climate. Withdrawal symptoms are tolerated with mild forms of habituation. The vast majority of betel-nut chewers are in this category, which is largely unassociated with serious mental health hazards. With the passage of time, predisposed personality types discover that the stresses and strains of life, insufficient food, and chronic illness become supportable with the aid of the chew. It becomes absolutely essential for sustained work, and the true addict needs a continuity of supplies. When these run out, he is compelled to abandon what he is doing in order to replenish his supply. He may lose his job, but the hardened chewer would rather risk that than give up his *buai*. He tends to swallow his saliva to a much greater extent than the ordinary betel-nut chewer, thus absorbing more arecoline, which is the active principle producing the stimulating effect. Addiction, as I have described it here, is uncommon. Betel-nut psychosis is even rarer. It occurs in the chronic user who has not been chewing for some time but who partakes heavily on a social occasion. It is characterized by auditory hallucinations and grandiose delusions and is acute and reversible.

If we are to assess the clinical situation solely on the standard nosological groupings, psychiatry as practiced in Papua New Guinea would appear at first sight in many ways similar to that practiced elsewhere, and the range of disease entities not unlike that of the developed country. We may also assume that the basic mental mechanisms brought to the conflict situation are essentially the same everywhere. The psychiatrist soon recognizes the need to reinterpret and redefine a number of factors, among which may be included the concepts of normality and abnormality, language, custom, and social organization.

The first difficulty for the psychiatrist is that of definition. What constitutes normality and abnormality in the transcultural context? How does one differentiate mental disorder from criminality? The definition I have found to be most useful is the following, although it may not be applicable in all instances: By the term *mental disorder* in Papua New Guinea I understand the individual's factual incapacity to conform to the role expectations of the cultural-linguistic group of which he is a member, irrespective of whether the incapacity originates from organic, psychogenic, or any other cause or combination of factors. If the patient has undergone a considerable degree of acculturation, then the role expectations of a wider social group will need to be taken into account, although it must be remembered that acculturation acts differentially on different cultural elements, some being more refractory to change than others. If we are able to separate psychiatric symptom from cultural norm clearly, without confusing the two—and this is no mean feat for the culture-bound alien—we are then in a position to show whether the symptomatology corresponds to known nosological entities as well, in which case the labels of European classificatory systems can be safely used. The key word is *incapacity*. Has the patient factual capacity to conform to the role expectations? If he is able to conform and does not do so, social control mechanisms may become operative, and if his conduct is antisocial, it will be categorized as criminal. If he is not able to conform, taking into account all the circumstances of the case, his behavior is undoubtedly pathologic. In the former instance, I prefer to use the term *facultative nonconformity*, in the latter *obligatory nonconformity*. Psychiatric skill is undoubtedly of value in both cases.

Another outstanding difficulty is that of communication. Not all communications of psychiatric import are necessarily mediated through the mechanism of language. Culturally modified emotional expressions and gestures play their part and are discussed elsewhere (Burton-Bradley 1967). As we have already noted, however, there are hundreds of different languages. The examiner will have little opportunity of learning the local *place talk*, as it is called, unless he stays in a given area for a considerable length of time. A lingua franca, such as Police Motu or Neomelanesian pidgin, is used. It is sometimes necessary to seek the aid of interpreters, to hospitalize the patient and observe his behavior over a period, and to make use of corroborative evidence when this is possible. Neomelanesian pidgin is undoubtedly most valuable, and it is the major language of psychiatry at the present time. It has developed out of the culture-contact situation and is spreading widely without any intervention on the part of the white Caucasian.

Customary behavior has to be recognized. The psychiatrist must know the norm. If he does not know it, he must seek this information from whatever source is available —anthropological studies, patrol reports, state hospital records, the patient's kin, and in some instances from the patient himself. Continually one is met with the explanation, "It's a village custom." Thus when one sees two young Mekeo males with hibiscus blossoms in their hair walking hand in hand along the main street of a large town, they are not necessarily homosexual, nor is the angry-looking Papuan woman who talks in a shrill excited manner suffering from a manic state. She does this all the time. Systems of sorcery are also well developed and can be of considerable value in therapy. Only occasionally is opportunity afforded the European-trained therapist to consult and confer with the sorcerer held responsible for any particular mental disorder. When a round-table conference of psychiatrist, patient, and sorcerer can be set up, a powerful combination is available and can lead to rapid recoveries. More usually, access to the sorcerer is difficult, and in these cases it is often possible to recruit the patient's relatives for negotiation. For a material consideration, such as an axe, a knife, or a few dollars, the sorcerer may be prevailed upon to remove the spell. When such information is conveyed to the patient, reduction of anxiety is obvious. Finally, the traditional practitioner, who may or may not be a sorcerer, is often in the background. The patient's attitude toward such a person cannot be ignored.

Some knowledge of the social organization or network of interpersonal relationships binding the people together socially is necessary. By and large, the microcultural-linguistic units are egalitarian and stateless in character, in contrast to the larger pyramidal types more common in some parts of Africa. There is very little authority. There has always been the so-called "big man," but his power to make judgments or settle disputes has seldom been strong. Because of the small size of Papua New Guinea societies, interpersonal kinship ties are of great importance, as are also the tensions inevitably arising from them. Thus one may be confronted with nondischarge of kinship obligations, pig killing, sorcery, adultery, homicide, violation of incest taboos, transgression of lactational and postpartum sex taboos, and stealing. These are subjects that should always be looked into as part of the examination.

What, then, are the present status and future prospects of the mental-health service with the emergence of new problems? There is a small but highly dedicated group of workers made up of psychiatrists, clinical psychologists, psychiatric social workers, psychiatric nurses, and a clinical anthropologist who maintain contact with all parts of the country through visits, telephone, and radio. Today there is a sophisticated range of technical treatment procedures similar to that of developed countries, although on a smaller scale, and suitably modified for adjustment to local cultural circumstances.

It is well recognized that insufficiency of funds and negative attitudes toward mental illness are the two most important factors in slowing down progress in the mental-health field, including prevention. Major action programs in operation are directed toward the tactics of mental-health education and promotion; medicopolitics; and the law as an instrument of prophylaxis, transcultural psychiatric research, and a sound system of formal services based on social realities rather than on the preferred fashions of our day.

Experience has shown that service, teaching, and research activities that deny or ignore the cultural variable are doomed to failure. Accordingly research is being applied to the study of acculturation stresses under conditions of rapid social change; customary beliefs and attitudes toward mental disorder; the traditional practitioner and the feasibility or infeasibility of his syncretistic integration into the superimposed alien medical system; the effects of certain classes of exogenous media on the minds of partially acculturated young people; the psychiatric implications of cargo cult and its analogues; and epidemiological surveys. It is abundantly clear that these should be long-term investigations and should employ interdisciplinary techniques, including a fusion of ethnographic and psychiatric principles.

References

Adams, A. R. D. 1951. Amok. In *British encyclopaedia of medical practice*, 2d ed. London: Butterworth & Company.

Burridge, K. O. L. 1960. *Mambu: a Melanesian millenium*. London: Methuen & Company.

Burton-Bradley, B. G. 1967. *Some aspects of South Pacific ethnopsychiatry*. Technical Paper 156. Nouméa, New Caledonia: South Pacific Commission.

————. 1970. The New Guinea prophet: Is the cultist always normal? *Med. J. Australia* 1:124–129.

————. 1973. *Longlong! Transcultural psychiatry in Papua New Guinea*. Port Moresby: Public Health Department.

Carothers, J. C. 1953. *The African mind in health and disease*. Geneva: World Health Organization monograph.

Dickie-Clark, H. F. 1966. *The marginal situation*. London: Routledge & Kegan Paul.

Durkheim, E. 1897. *Le Suicide: étude de sociologie*. Paris: Alcan.

————. 1952. *Suicide*. London: Routledge & Kegan Paul.

Fitzgerald, R. D. 1923. A thesis on two tropical neuroses (amok and latah) peculiar to Malaya. In *Transactions of the fifth biennial congress*, Far Eastern Association for Tropical Medicine, Singapore.

Fortune, R. 1932. *The sorcerers of Dobu*. London: Routledge & Kegan Paul.

Gaikwad, V. R. 1970. Personal communication.

Galloway, D. J. 1923. On amok. In *Transactions of the fifth biennial congress*, Far Eastern Association for Tropical Medicune, Singapore.

Gimlette, J. D. Notes on a case of amok, *J. Trop. Med.* 4:195–96.

119

Hook, S. 1955. *The hero in history: a study in limitation and possibility*. Boston: Beacon Press.

Hoskin, J. O.; Friedman, M. I.; and Cawte, J. 1969. A high incidence of suicide in a preliterate-primitive society. *Psychiatry* 32:200–210.

Hwekmarin, L.; Jamenan, J.; and Lea, D. 1971. Yangoru cargo cult. *J. Papua New Guinea Soc.* 5:3–27.

Kerckhoff, A. C., and McCormick, T. C. 1955. Marginal status and marginal personality. *Social Forces* 34:48–55.

Kiki, Albert M. 1968. *Ten thousand years in a lifetime*. Melbourne: F. W. Cheshire.

Lawrence, P. 1964. *Road belong cargo*. Melbourne: Melbourne University Press.

Leeson, I. 1952. *Bibliographie des "cargo cults" et autres mouvements autochthones du Pacific Sud*. Nouméa, New Caledonia: South Pacific Commission.

Legge, J. D. 1955. *Australian colonial policy—a survey of native administration and European development in Papua*. Sydney: Angus & Robertson.

L'Etang, H. 1969. *The pathology of leadership*. London: William Heinemann Medical Books.

Lett, L. 1949. *Sir Hubert Murray of Papua*. London: William Collins Sons.

Lewin, K. 1952. *Field theory in social science*. London: Tavistock Publications.

Maher, R. F. 1961. *New man of Papua: a study of culture change*. Madison: University of Wisconsin Press.

Malinowski, B. 1959. *Crime and custom in savage society*. Totowa, New Jersey: Littlefield, Adams & Company.

Masters, W. E. 1920. *Essentials of tropical medicine*. London: John Bale and Danielsson.

Monckton, C. A. W. 1921. *Experiences of a New Guinea resident magistrate*. London: John Lane the Bodley Head.

Park. R. E. 1928. Human migration and the marginal man. *Amer. J. Sociology* 33:881–893.

Parker, N., and Burton-Bradley, B. G. 1966. Suicide in Papua and New Guinea. *Med. J. Australia* 2:1125–1128.

Pospisil, L. J. 1958. *Kapauku Papuans and their law*. New Haven, Connecticut: Yale University Publications in Anthropology.

Schwartz, T. 1962. *The Paliau movement in the Admiralty Islands, 1946–1953.* New York: American Museum of Natural History Anthropological Papers.

Scragg, R. F. R. 1966. Personal communication.

Smith, A. G. 1957. *Bibliography of koro, amok, and latah.* Atlanta, Georgia: Emory University Department of Sociology.

Stanhope, J. H. 1966. Personal communication.

Stonequist, E.V. 1937. *The marginal man.* New York: Charles Scribner's Sons.

Thurnwald, R. C. 1929. Papuanisches und Melanisches geboitsndlich des Aquators einschliesslich Neuguinea. In *Das Eigenborenenrecht,* Vol. 2. Stuttgart.

Todd, J. A. 1935–36. Redress of wrongs in South West New Britain. *Oceania* 6:401–441.

Tumin, M. 1945. Some fragments from the life history of a marginal man. *Character and Personality* 13:261–296.

White, L. 1949. *The science of culture: a study of man and civilization.* New York: Farrar, Straus and Giroux.

Williams, F. E. 1923. *The vailala madness and the destruction of native ceremonies.* Anthropological Report No. 4. Port Moresby: Government Printer.

————. 1934. The vailala madness in retrospect. In *Essays Presented to C. G. Seligman,* ed. E. E. Evans-Pritchard. London: Kegan Paul.

————, ed. 1939. The reminiscences of Ahuia Ova. *Journal of the Royal Anthropological Institute* 64:11–14.

————. 1941. *Natives of Lake Kutubu.* Sydney: Oceania Monograph No. 6, p. 70.

Worsley, P. 1968. *The trumpet shall sound: a study of "cargo" cults in Melanesia,* 2d ed. New York: Schocken Books.

Wulfften-Palthe, P. M. van. 1933. Amok. *Med J. Geneesk* 7:983–989.

Index

Abau, Central District: case of amok from, 56
Abnormality: defining, 115
Achievement, 110-111
Adams, A. R. D., 51
Addiction. *See* Drugs
Adolescence, 91-93
Adultery: as a consideration in psychiatric examination, 117
Affective incongruity: as a schizophrenic sign, 109
Affective psychosis. *See* Psychosis, affective
Africa: amok in, 50-51
Aggression: in a marginal situation, 104; as a result of schizophrenia, 110
Alcohol. *See* Drinking
Aliens, 46
Amnesia: accompanying amok, 50, 55, 57, 59, 63
Amok, 6, 18, 50-68; as a means of suicide, 36, 44; incidence of, 51-52; description of, 52-53; case studies of, 54-62; in "foreigners," 56, 58; in Caucasians, 60-62; diagnosis of, 63-65; legal responsibility for actions during, 65-66; prevention of, 68
Amputation. *See* Self-amputation
Anger, 110-111
Anomie, 48
Anxiety, 110-111, 113; cargo, 16; in a marginal situation, 104
Arawa: location of a major general hospital, 108
Arecoline: stimulant in betel nut, 114

Aroma: girls "passing" as mixed-race, 103
Australia, 70-71
Australian law, 41. *See also* Queensland Criminal Code
Australians, 46
Automaniacs, 13
Awa'awa, 5

Badili: a separate mixed-race community, 73; lack of racial tension in, 78
Bahasia Indonesia (language), 5
Baigona cult, 18
Behavior, self-destructive, 48
Betel intoxication, 54
Betel nut, 114
Blackwood (explorer), 70
Bomana: hospital at, 27, 107; separate mixed-race community, 73
Boroko, 74
Boroko Psychiatric Clinic and Mental Health Headquarters, 108
Bougainville (explorer), 70
Bougainville (island): copper project on, 4; patients from, 16, 27
Breast feeding, 91
Bridewealth practice, 80, 86
Buai, 114
Burridge, K. O. L., 14
Burton-Bradley, B. G. (joint author), 35, 108, 116

Cargo anxiety. *See* Anxiety, cargo
Cargo cult, 6, 10-31, 44, 118; local coloring, 10; Vailala Madness, 13; dreams

123